Girls, Social Class, and Literacy

What Teachers Can Do to Make a Difference

Stephanie Jones

Foreword by Randy Bomer

HEINEMANN
Portsmouth, NH

Heinemann

361 Hanover Street
Portsmouth, NH 03801–3912
www.heinemann.com

Offices and agents throughout the world

The author and publisher wish to thank those who have generously given permission to reprint borrowed material:

Portions of Chapter 4, "Taboo No More: Validating Lives on the Margins," originally appeared as "Living Poverty and Literacy Learning: Sanctioning the Topics of Students' Lives" by Stephanie Jones in *Language Arts* 81(6), 461–489. Copyright © 2004 by the National Council of Teachers of English. Reprinted with permission.

Library of Congress Cataloging-in-Publication Data
Jones, Stephanie.
  Girls, social class, and literacy : what teachers can do to make a difference / Stephanie Jones ; foreword by Randy Bomer.
     p. cm.
  Includes bibliographical references and index.
  ISBN-13: 978-0-325-00840-0
  ISBN-10: 0-325-00840-X
  1. Educational sociology—United States—Case studies. 2. Girls—Education—United States—Case studies. 3. Education, Urban—United States—Case studies. 4. Critical pedagogy—United States—Case studies. I. Title.
  LC191.J665 2006
  371.822—dc22   2006020001

Acquisitions Editor: Lois Bridges
Editor: Gloria Pipkin
Production service: Denise Botelho
Production coordinator: Patricia Adams
Cover design: Night & Day Design
Cover photograph: Joanie
Typesetter: Tom Allen, Pear Graphic Design
Manufacturing: Steve Bernier

Printed in the United States of America on acid-free paper
10   09   VP   3   4   5

*This book is dedicated to my mother
and our family's rich pasts and presents.*

*And to Johnathan, Madisyn, and Hayden,
our promising futures.*

Contents

Foreword
Vulnerability and Achievement

Many U.S. citizens think of their country as a land of opportunity—a place where people can create a good life for themselves and their children. Everyone can get a living, and everyone can get an education. It is a promise we collectively make to ourselves, even though it is often a hard one really to achieve. We see evidence of that difficulty year after year, when reports come out about a gap in academic achievement between various ethnic and economic groups.

In recent years, politicians have made law and policy out of their impatience with this state of affairs. The law sometimes known as "No Child Left Behind" has many serious faults, but it also carries the nearly radical message that it is intolerable for schools to write off poor and minority children as necessary losses. The requirement that schools report the scores of various ethnic groups, as well as low-income children, has shone a bright light on American schools, and it suggests that they are not necessarily the places of open and fair opportunity that we would like to think they are. Consequently, schools all over the country are scrambling to find ways of raising the test scores of disadvantaged students.

If they do not raise those scores, the adults in the schools face public humiliation or other uncomfortable sanctions, and so they search for answers out of their fear and anxiety. Fear does not, however, create an environment in which people are likely to look closely at children in order to understand them. The standards and testing regime, rather, sets a bar and asks a binary question as to whether or not individuals make the grade. The question is simply *are the kids good enough at the tasks we have authorized?* The question is not *who are these children now and who are they becoming?* but *What world have we created for them, and how does their learning reflect or improve that world?* The language of most current education reform does not even permit such questions to be posed. There is little effort, then, to understand the lives and characters of low-income children, only to fix the parts of them that are substandard, as measured on a test, to make them less of a problem for adults, to get them to conform to a strictly enforced image, however fictional, of what is normal, middle-class, and economically productive.

Stephanie Jones's book speaks into this context, allowing readers a deeper-than-usual look at the lives and thoughts of a few students from low-income households. Based in ethnographic research, the book shows, with great respect, the struggles and strengths of a handful of elementary-age girls and their mothers. Mindful that she is representing some of the most vulnerable people in society, poor female children, Jones treats her informants with admiration, caring, and a sense of identification. She is interested in how they grow as students, but she sees that academic growth as integrated into the whole person, the whole life. In showing us these girls in this way, she humanizes the way we look at students like them—helping us see such children not as demographic categories but as unique individuals who share a position created for them by powerful social and economic interests.

We teachers want and need to hear what Stephanie Jones has to say to us, because every time we interact with a student, we act like we know whom we are talking to. We enact a story in which we, as teacher, are one particular character, and the student is another particular character. With poor students, these imagined stories we play out may be ones in which the students' homes and families are defective and dysfunctional when compared with our own. They may be stories in which we are awed by the drama in the children's lives. The narrative may be one in which we are rescuers or safe havens, providers or role models. Such narratives are ready-made in the culture, and we sometimes substitute them for the reality of interactions. When we take on these narratives and likewise position children to take on complementary roles, we create identities and interactions that may not always match up to lived reality. It is important that we have evidence-based accounts, detailed and three-dimensional ones, of the lives of children whose families struggle economically, in order to counteract the powerful stories we think we know, from television and other media, and from the lies our culture has made a habit of telling about the poor for two centuries.

In the nineteenth and early twentieth centuries, it was common to think of the poor as being in their economic condition because they were genetically defective. People were thought to be poor because of their lower quality of character, their intrinsic feeblemindedness, debauchery, and laziness—and such words were common in the language used to describe them. The causes of poverty were assumed to be in the individual, rather than in a social system structured to be unequal, designed to repress some people's wealth and income in order to grow that of others. Beliefs about the poor were often explicitly tied to eugenics, the project of improving humanity through breeding people with the most desirable qualities. Eugenics was not limited to Nazism, but was considered by many to be a valid scientific program throughout the world, particularly in the United States. After the liberation of the concentration camps in Europe, however, both eugenics and genetic accounts of deficit were mostly discredited and abandoned.

Deficit perspectives later in the twentieth century turned to the idea of culture to explain what was "wrong" with the poor. According to this cultural deficit perspective, poverty produced a culture that was entirely separate from that of the middle class. The poor were thought to participate in a way of life that was noisy, messy, chaotic, sexualized, criminal, violent, distrustful of authority, fatalistic, and hedonistic. The families, assumed to be matriarchal, were dysfunctional and were the main agency transmitting undesirable qualities across generations. Schools were, naturally, handed the responsibility of fixing poor children, instilling in them middle class values so that they could move up, while underlying economic relations creating poverty were left as they were. Adopting a deficit perspective, then, was a way of blaming the victim.

Apparently, it is too painful to think that individuals who are economically disadvantaged are just like the ones who are economically advantaged: created equal and still equal, morally and spiritually as valuable, working as hard to make a living and to make their lives satisfying and meaningful, and as deserving of happiness and full well-being. It is more comfortable to think that others' misfortune is a result of something that the individual could have avoided, like learning that a traffic accident was a result of recklessness. Better that the poor should be people who are nonverbal, or whose language is deficient, or whose attitudes and cognition are different, or who really asked for it all along. Fictions like a deficit perspective make it possible to think that oppression, like privilege, is deserved. It is a fiction that makes justice irrelevant.

Recently, this deficit perspective has been on the rise again, as schools respond to pressures to raise the achievement of low-income students. Certain professional development programs have made millions of dollars by convincing teachers and administrators of a deficit view of their students. The instructional program that results is usually focused on changing behavior and language patterns, as if learning a code or a register will make up for the lack of material resources that separates the poor from economically better lives. Too rarely is there any attention to students' legitimate connection to the lives they currently live and the relationships that give those lives meaning. Too rarely is there any sense that children should not be as poor as they are, that society could and should take better care of them so that they won't be hungry. There are too few conversations about the proposition that middle class teachers have a role to play in advocating for children, either one by one or through legislation and funding. And too seldom is there any suggested way of approaching conversations with the students themselves about the systems of inequality and injustice that make life difficult for them and their families, about the systems that create poverty and concentrate it in certain groups or neighborhoods. These silences poison an important conversation about children's lives, families' values, and America's future that needs to happen in place of a fixation on an "achievement gap" manifest in test scores.

Stephanie Jones's book provides an antidote to that poison. Focusing on a group of particular girls from economically vulnerable families, Jones's data address specific life stories, not generalities about class and race. It is a small study, focused on a town, a gender, a socioeconomic location, an age cohort, a circle of acquaintance. Jones only researched girls. The poverty she witnessed was particular to a specific location and was undoubtedly different from the lives of the families she now must see in New York City. But looking this closely permits us to see that each of these girls, and each of these mothers of girls, contains multitudes. No one is just a gender, a class, or a race. Each person enacts diverse identities. What might look like a monolith—*children of poverty*—is really an intricate mosaic of different attitudes, behaviors, capacities, and experiences. I cannot know anything about an abstract category like *children of poverty*. Jones's writing makes me realize the degree to which my preexisting categories can cause me to miss the real children in front of me. The only appropriate relationship to these children is curiosity, wonder, and interest, rather than the certainty that I already know something about them once I know their parents' incomes. I realize that I have to learn an intellectual and interpersonal humility, a willingness to learn. As a teacher, I need to pay attention to the ways Jones went about learning about these students, and the meanings she made of what she discovered.

Stephanie Jones uses herself—her own life history and memory—as an instrument of investigation. Having grown up in a low-income family, she makes herself vulnerable first by teaching from that experience, and second, by writing about it. But this is a vulnerability more powerful than strength. Her family was much more than simply low-income, and she can see their strength as clearly as she sees the resources they did without. Her use of memory makes her wise, resistant to nonsense, and capable of interpreting the human narratives she sees and hears. She identifies with these girls, and that identification multiplies the information from which she can draw. Some people who write about children from low-income families act as if all teachers identify with the middle class, but many of us came from working class or poor families. It is common for teachers to be the first in their families to attend or finish college. Jones shows us how to use what we know in order to become insiders in our students' neighborhoods and lives, how to create common ground with students who are distant from our present selves but no so far from the people we were—and those we loved—when we were children. She shows us, too, a possible way to begin talking about poverty with children who are themselves poor, though they may not introduce themselves as being from such a social category. For most teachers, such conversations are hard to imagine having, and it helps to have guides like Stephanie Jones help us picture how it might go, even though we know it might still feel awkward and difficult, and even though we know our own students will respond differently from hers. New kinds of classroom conversations, about literacy or about social class, arise out of images in our mind's eye of how such conversations might go, and Jones provides such an image.

Among books and articles about poverty and education, Jones's book is also distinguished by its social hope. She is not content to leave the world's inequalities where they are, but wants to teach students to understand how systems of power and privilege work, to recognize and critique them, to question and confront their effects. The book includes some of the questions that might help classrooms approach a critical form of literacy—a way of reading that is oriented toward making the world more fair and just. These are important steps toward a literacy curriculum in the interest of a world that is more attentive to the voices, needs, and experiences of the most vulnerable.

In education these days, "achievement" is an important word, but it usually refers to test scores, a spiritless concept not worthy of teachers' energies and ambitions. The achievement Stephanie Jones focuses on is the achievement of a world in which her students become citizens for whom children living in poverty, silence, and passivity is unacceptable. In a democracy's school system, that is an achievement for which we should all be striving.

—RANDY BOMER

Acknowledgments

This book grew out of my dissertation research under the guidance of a dedicated advisor, Deborah Hicks, and committee members Rhoda Halperin, Annette Hemmings, Barbara Comber, and Patricia O'Reilly, five women to whom I am indebted for helping me to grow as a researcher, writer, scholar, and activist—thank you. The Spencer Foundation provided funding for this research and I cannot thank them enough for the gift of time, a luxury I had not experienced before receiving the Spencer Dissertation Fellowship. My deepest gratitude goes to each person who waded through early drafts of chapters: Deborah Hicks, Barbara Comber, Lesley Bartlett, Lalitha Vasudevan, Rebecca Rogers, Jen Thiel, Cathy Compton-Lilly, Emily Skinner, Rhoda Halperin, Deborah Anderson, Grace Enriquez, my 2005–2006 students at Teachers College, Columbia University, and my mother, thank you for your patience and feedback that guided me toward better thinking and writing. Lane Clarke and Karen Spector, my dear friends who read and responded to many chapters, thank you for your honesty, energy, and encouragement throughout the process of writing this book; your voices have no doubt found their way into the lines on these pages, but I am solely responsible for any and all shortcomings in the text. And to my editor and new friend, Gloria Pipkin, your words pushed and pulled me along every step of the way; thank you for believing in me.

Unlike most people I know, naming aunts, uncles, great-aunts, great-uncles, first, second, and third cousins, and grandmothers back three generations is something that comes easy to me and most others in my family. There is a long history in my mother's family of knowing, supporting, and loving every person on the family tree. This history is from where I write, and though it would take pages to acknowledge each family member who has contributed to my well-being and my thinking about the world, I want to acknowledge them as a group: Thank you with all my heart.

Mom, you are my hero and my most important teacher—thank you for your wisdom, devotion, and enthusiasm. Thank you to my brother John, for standing with me through thick and thin, good times and bad, and for always questioning and challenging what is happening in our society. Thank you to my baby sister Desiree, who came along when I was a teenager and who has put up with my constant mothering ever since. I am indebted to all three of you for being patient as I rattled on and on about how the world needed to be changed, for correcting me when my perspective was too narrow, and for teaching me what unconditional love means. Thank you to George and Mark, my biological and adopted fathers, for calling to see how the book was coming; it means a lot to know that you were thinking about me and this writing. Thank you to my family through marriage, a father-in-law with a similar history as my own family, and a mother-in-law with insightful understandings of societal injustices, your words of encouragement have meant a great deal. And to my maternal grandmother who is the leader of our enormous extended family, words cannot express the inspiration you provide for me and everyone around you. I hope to some day have a fraction of your strength, determination, resilience, and intuition. And finally, to my husband Casey and my daughter Hayden who spent many daddy-daughter days together as I stared at the computer screen wondering why I decided to write a book; your presence, smiles, and love make everything worthwhile.

I cannot thank enough everyone at Bruger Elementary School and in the community of St. Francis who welcomed me with open arms and talked honestly and openly with me about deeply personal issues such as teaching, learning, and social class.

And finally, the precocious girls written into these pages, thank you for all that you have taught me; I am forever indebted to you and your families. Your tenderness and strength will stay with me forever; I honor you and hope the words on these pages convey the richness of your minds and lives.

Introduction

Class and culture erect boundaries that hinder our vision—blind us to the logic of error and the everpresent stirring of language—and encourage the designation of otherness, difference, deficiency.

—Mike Rose, *Lives on the Boundary*

Each of them had been considered At Risk at one time or another, all of them were thought to have hard family lives, and some of the eight girls in this study already knew how other people perceived them. Perceptions of students from working-poor families are often formed through vision that has been "hindered" as Mike Rose puts it, a narrow seeing that encourages middle-class people to designate children and families as other, different, and deficient. Boundaries erected by class and culture are in desperate need of being deconstructed, taken apart one assumption or stereotype at a time. My brief introductions of the girls will begin with a descriptor that might have been used by a school official, and then I will add one layer to complicate the dominant perception. Two layers, however, only begin to tell the story of each of these feisty and beautiful, sweet and angry, loud and articulate, insightful and manipulative girls. But it will at least initiate the process of seeing and acknowledging the many parts, or "identities," of all students and considering these from multiple perspectives.

Fair-skinned, blue-eyed Alexis might be considered the quiet one in this bunch, but then I would be shortchanging her rambunctious and inquisitive sides that she demonstrated around the neighborhood by squealing her bike tires, climbing trees, and closely studying dead cats that were found regularly during her second grade year.

Chocolate-skinned, dark soulful-eyed Faith might be described as the happy-go-lucky girl in this book, but then I would be ignoring her sermons around right and wrong according to the Bible, her tendency to compare her younger sister to the Devil, and the pain she felt after her father's accident at work when his legs stopped working and the wheelchair took over.

Long-, dark-haired Sarah may be thought of as a teacher's pet, but that performance was limited to the hearing range of the teacher and changed dramatically when the teacher wasn't around and Sarah would challenge a lesson presented, such as one on bullying when Sarah said, "It ain't fair to call someone a bully."

Thin, fair, and dyed-blond-haired Rose could be considered the troubled girl who screamed, cried, and sat silent too often, but then I would be downplaying the joyful part of her who played house with her cousins, worked at a corner store with her grandma, and wrote about her mother "the angel" in her life.

Heather might be called the princess, prancing around on tiptoes during choice time with a paper-made crown atop her long blond-haired head, but she also boasted, loudly, about kicking boys in the "hotdog."

Tangled-haired Cadence could be dubbed the Bad Girl in the group, turning her back to the teacher and screaming "No!" from across the room, but this wouldn't capture the kindness she exhibited at home with her mom, grandma, and grandpa as she kissed them, helped them clean, and stood beside them learning to cook.

Black-haired, freckle-skinned Joanie might be the attitude girl, hand-on-hip and head swaying back and forth as she tells a peer what she can do with herself, but I would be ignoring her deep desire for academic achievement and her consistent push for equality in the classroom—characteristics that would indeed make her a good lawyer, as her mother pointed out.

And Joanie's cousin, Callie, might be considered the least likely to succeed given that her teachers had already "failed" her one year, but cold-eyed, stone-faced Callie wept as she read poetry, journaled with her mother at home, and became the master of the group with manipulating digital photographs.

The lives of these eight young girls, Joanie, Callie, Sarah, Faith, Cadence, Rose, Heather, and Alexis, their classmates, and their families will be peppered throughout this book. Their lives have become a part of my own as I engaged in this research since the girls' first day of first grade, following them through the fifth grade.[1] Their worlds have seeped into my subconscious much like the lives of my own family members, and I hope they will seep into yours. Another life that is a part of this book is my own, one that mirrors the girls' and their mothers' in many ways, but took a different turn in early adulthood as I became the first college graduate in my family and began taking baby steps toward a more privileged, but complicated, middle-class existence.

Lives are complex and created through experiences of the social structures around us including social class, a concept that will be foregrounded in this book. Class and poverty in the United States and how working poverty is lived in a predominantly White urban enclave by seven White girls and one African American girl and their families will be explored. How class is felt, lived, constructed, articulated, understood, and resisted in complex, even contradictory ways grounds the text to build a solid foundation challenging stereotypical notions of urban poverty. I challenge readers to consider how the "War on Poverty" in President Johnson's era became the "War Against the Poor" (Gans 1995) that continues today as people living in poverty are systemically and socially discriminated against because of their material living conditions and their economic, linguistic, social, and cultural capital that cannot be easily exchanged for privilege and opportunity in a world that operates like a market (Bourdieu 1991, 1992, 1994).

Lives are also created through literacy practices, and what I will refer to as *critical literacy* in this book will serve as an important foundation from which to critically read interactions inside and outside school as well as texts that perpetuate stereotypes and assumptions. Reading, writing, and language, in the broadest sense, will be used to look at the ways educators understand children and families, how families and children understand educators, and how language learning spaces in the classroom can include and build upon experiences of working-class and poor children in valuable, validating, and powerful ways. Transformative education that invites students to attach themselves to school without rejecting their family or shedding identities they've formed within their community will be an important part of this literacy work. Such work in the classroom, however, could not be possible without the in-depth understanding of *lives* and the ways in which class, gender, and race come together to shape the social, psychological, physical, and academic lives of the young people with whom we work.

Lives are created through identities and the experiences of shaping, resisting, performing, and negotiating identities across various social, psychological, and physical landscapes. The girls in this study lived in homes with strong values and beliefs that were intertwined with their material lives and social class and gender positionings. As they crossed the threshold of school they were faced with adhering to the strong values and beliefs held by teachers, principals, counselors, and others within the bureaucracy who are closely connected to the material lives of more dominant classes. The social class divide is a large and deep one, and one that may be felt more by school-aged children than by anyone else as their identities are challenged, punished, or even used as examples of how *not* to be successful in our society. Perhaps more than men or women working with others of similar social class status, working-class and poor students are reminded daily of their difference from what is valued in the larger society (hooks 1996; Rist 2000; Santiago 1993; Walkerdine 1998; Walkerdine, Lucey, and Melody 2001). Their understanding of classed identities within the educational and justice system begins quite young and will be demonstrated in this book as young as first grade.

Like the lives within these pages, your life, too, has been constructed through your experiences with social structures, literacy practices, and identity work. You, the educator who is committed to teaching students and building relationships with families, the educator who chose the profession to make a difference, the educator who believes that public schooling in the United States can be a vehicle of mobility for children from working-class and poor communities, will also be a part of this book. This book is written to help you reflect on yourself as a reader, a writer, and a literacy educator. You will be invited to work through exercises and think deeply about narratives I share; I hope collaborative work with colleagues will support you in this undertaking as we try, together, to build more sensitive and productive ways of talking with and about children and families who have been marginalized since the beginning of public education. Together we will work toward serving our students and their families in their best interest through literacy.

Let yourself linger a bit with this book without expecting quick fixes. Make explicit and deliberate connections and disconnections between the text and your personal life, your classroom life, and the life you would like to live. Work toward moving beyond this book as you use it as a window of opportunity through which to imagine what might be possible for you and the children and families you serve.

■ Note

1   The girls will begin their sixth-grade year as this book is released.

Where Are We From?
A Look into Ourselves

1

Mrs. Stritt was my fourth grade teacher and a skilled clogger. Her salt-and-pepper curls bounced around her enthusiastic, wrinkled face as she urged me to follow along clap-clacking my toes and heels. Sliding and clicking my dance shoes to "Rocky Top" and other traditional mountain songs felt good, comfortable. As our clogging group improved Mrs. Stritt entered us into dance competitions and a weekend rehearsal was called. On a chilly, sunny Saturday morning my mom and stepdad drove me to my teacher's home. Stepping outside our van, I stopped in mid-stride and stared with awe at her house: the newly constructed two-story brick house sat on a grassy slope with manicured landscaping and an inground pool. Having never seen such a house in real life, I was nervous about entering. Coaxed by my mom, I walked up the steps and crossed the threshold into my emerging consciousness of social class.

It all started right there on the periphery of Mrs. Stritt's middle-class property; the world that opened up to me that morning made my head spin and the years ahead of me complicated things even more. Even as I sit down to write this book I am not certain that I have a solid grasp on how and why social class differences are turned into opportunities for judgment and discrimination, but I am certain that my personal life, coupled with research and literature, has taught me a great deal about this dirty little secret of the Land of the Free. Classism in America has a long history and painful realities, and where we are from paints a picture of what we believe about class.

■ Where Are You From?

We are each a part of a complex history that includes our experiences and expectations, family structures and friendship circles, powerful achievements and marginalized realities. Our locations in this world color the lenses through which we read it. Yes—we *read* the world. Reading, whether reading the world or written words, is impacted by what our lives are and what they have been.

"Where are you from?" is a loaded question many of us encounter as we meet new people, travel to new places, or begin conversations with strangers in public spaces. For those of us who are from places that are considered to be the wrong side of the tracks, this question is always one of uncertainty. Sandra Cisneros writes:

> You live there? There. I had to look to where she pointed—the third floor, the paint peeling, wooden bars Papa had nailed on the windows so we wouldn't fall out. You live there? The way she said it made me feel like nothing. There. I lived there. (2001, 27)

Those of us from all the *theres* in this world know that we skate on thin ice when such questions are asked: Is today the day I answer with honesty and dignity—or will I answer broadly and vaguely with names of large cities or neighboring communities? How will this person judge me if I'm honest? Do I care about how this person judges me? A question many people don't think twice about often causes great anxiety for others, including myself. The place we are *from* is often code for social class affiliation and though we don't talk specifically about that, most of us know it. We are from more than physical places, however, we are from people, food, objects, language, religion, recreation, institutions—and together these form our beliefs about how the world works. Where, who, and what we are from is a critical part of how we read written texts and the world around us.

I wrote the following poem in front of my second grade students on the first day of school modeling it after George Ella Lyon's *where i'm from* (1999) poem. It is short and simple, and could even be read as "quaint" but we will use it to move toward a critical analysis of how our complex histories construct what we believe to be "normal."

I am from shooing cigarette smoke,
I am from haircuts on the porch,
    snip, snip, snip.
I am from rain dropping on

my tin roof
   singing me a lullaby.
I am from reading books on
   cold, snowy days.
I am from writing sitting on
   concrete steps.

Exercise 1.1 Where I'm From

1. Write for ten minutes starting each line with "I am from . . ."
2. Read your writing aloud.
3. Use one or two of the following prompts and continue writing for ten additional minutes:
   Am I from a place?
   Certain words or phrases?
   Smells?
   Objects?
   Experiences that made me feel special?
   Experiences that made me feel different?
4. When the second ten minutes has ended, read your writing to yourself or someone nearby.

How does each of your lines affect assumptions you might hold about the world around you? For example, if you wrote that you are from a mother cooking dinner while dad read the newspaper on the deck—what kind of family structure do you consider normal? Let's analyze the poem that I modeled after *where i'm from* for my second grade students.

As a young child and maturing adolescent, my experience with smoking family members helped to create my assumption that most adults smoked. Period. Though the smoke irritated me, a smokeless home never occurred to me until I came into contact with friends' family members who did not smoke. I assumed that somehow their not smoking had something to do with money since those friends lived in single-family, owner-occupied homes—and I did not. A similar experience arose from my haircuts-on-the-porch history. Assuming that everyone's mother or father cut his or her hair at home, I was stunned to learn that well-groomed peers visited salons or barbershops on a regular basis to maintain their just-cut look. Again, money seemed to be the major difference here, since each of those peers had some and I had none.

The tin roof in my poem is the roof of a trailer. Raindrops hitting it comforted me on countless nights as I lay on my side, closed my eyes, and drifted to sleep. Most things in my trailer park comforted me in fact: loads of kids to play with, many families that cared for me, the security of the insular park itself that was shaped as a sun with a circular driving path and spoke-like dead end streets. The pond in the center of that sun pulled friends together to fish, look for snakes, and occasionally (without supervision) slide on the frozen surface in winter. The trailer park families formed a tight community that looked after children, babysat in emergency situations, came to the rescue during tragedies, and gathered in one yard or another on weekend evenings until the wee hours of the morning. This particular part of my childhood created assumptions early on that neighbors lived communally. I was shocked to learn otherwise, especially when I came to realize that many people shunned trailer park existence, and assumed (among other things) they were inhabited by "White Trash."

And finally, reading and writing. With a mother who read and kept journals, and three grandmothers who read newspapers, *Reader's Digest*, and popular culture magazines regularly, I assumed that most women were readers and writers. Though I didn't always read and write to complete assignments in school (yes, I was one of those students with so much potential and so little follow-through), I read and wrote for myself at home and I assumed most people did, or would if they had the time and opportunity.

In short, based only on one simple "where i'm from" poem, it's safe to say that I considered life in a trailer park with smoking adults, front porch haircuts, and reading and writing *normal* and even desirable. Normal people, to me, have lived similar lives and have had similar experiences. Struggling to make ends meet while ensuring fun time with the family is something I have always valued and continue to value as how most people live. At different times in my life it has been difficult for me to trust and respect people who haven't traversed economic hardships; it didn't seem normal, therefore it was suspect. My early conceptions of normal life continue to influence the way I read the world around me, but understanding these complexities also helps me to move beyond my world, to understand that there is an infinite number of normal experiences in our society, many differing from my own.

Exercise 1.2 Analyzing Your Poem

- What does your poem say about you?

- What are your assumptions about how the world works?

- What experiences do you consider normal?

Talk through your poem line-by-line and come to some understanding about how your experiences articulated in this exercise have colored the lenses through which you read the world around you.

Just as this chapter opened with a small window allowing you a peek into my girlhood, your poems serve as the same opportunity. Window peeks into lives through writing are always limited to what the author decides to include and exclude, but they are peeks nonetheless. Creating classroom spaces where such glimpses are made an official part of the literacy curriculum is critical, and I urge you to begin each school year with language and literacy engagements that will do three things:

1. Convince students that their lives are welcome and validated in the classroom
2. Invite students to engage their lived experiences within official literacy curricula
3. Offer you the opportunity to gain knowledge and insight about the lives of your students outside of school

Reading and composing *where i'm from* poems is only one possibility, and in the following section I will outline my experience with this activity while I was teaching second grade.[1] The context in which Lyon's poem was introduced is critical and described here but you are likely to find a similarly inviting text that is equally relevant to your students. Following the description of the classroom work around authors and texts, I analyze what I believe the girls (and all the students) were gaining from this particular experience and why it moved the classroom space toward more class-sensitive pedagogical practices.

■ Moving Toward *I Am From* on the First Day of School

Lori, a White single mother of three girls, including Cadence in this study, was never reluctant to share her philosophy of educating children. Sitting in her first-floor apartment of a three-family home that burned only weeks following this particular interview, Lori talked fast and furiously about children's lives:

> I think you come at them on their level—okay—and you let them express themselves at their own level—what they wanna express themselves about, *you* will have that child—you will. They will be just like a book, you can open them right up. You have to find what it is about them—and nine times out of ten, with kids it *is* their life.

Opening a child right up, as Lori put it, is quite a challenge given that many working-class and poor children[2] have already learned by first grade (as you will read in Chapter 4) that certain parts of their lives are not welcome in school. Starting with their lives, however, is a good way to begin the process.

▪ First Day of Second Grade

The first day of second grade was a scorcher. Late August in the Midwest can be miserable, and this day certainly fit the category. The hot sun peeked over the bridge in the distance and the river shimmered with orange and red hues. The view was too stunning to ignore, so the class and I decided to wait until the yellow disc was high in the sky before pulling the shades on the six tall windows across the east wall of the classroom. Following introductions of new students (most of them were in the same first grade classroom together), a good-morning song signed in American Sign Language, and a chance for each child to greet the class, we began our first author study of the year: Cynthia Rylant.

Cynthia Rylant, like many of the families of this community, St. Francis, is from the Appalachian Mountains. A number of her books are reminiscent of Rylant's childhood years in the mountains with her grandparents, pets, and extended family members. Beyond the introduction of memoir as a genre for writing, I wanted the students to begin to recognize the value of a humble, family-oriented existence, an existence that is often portrayed in caricature fashion such as *The Beverly Hillbillies* and used for repugnant jokes such as "You must be a redneck if . . . ."

As we discussed Rylant's *When I Was Young in the Mountains* (1982), we talked as a class about authors who use their lives for writing. I explicitly told the children that they, too, would be such authors. Following this discussion that was focused on the reading of texts to study an author's craft, I introduced a second author who uses her life to create beautiful poetry, George Ella Lyon (also from the Appalachian Mountains). I read aloud her poem *where i'm from* (1999, 3), pausing for effect and looking out from the book and into the children's eyes. The reading left wide-eyed second graders wondering about many of the words and images, and led the class into a lively conversation around where each of us was from.

Through modeled writing—or what I like to call "write alouds,"[3] I wrote my own poem using Lyon as my mentor for considering what kinds of things to include and how to begin each line (included in Exercise 1.1). People then talked with a partner and decided upon one line for themselves that would be added to a collaborative class poem:

We are from . . .
(modeled after George Ella Lyon)

I am from [St. Francis].
    I am from God.
        I am from Jesus.
I am from the clouds in the sky.
    I am from reading and writing.
        I am from Ohio.
I am from the sun.
    I am from New York.
        I am from going to my mom's.
I am from the angels.
    I am from Jesus, my friend.
        I am from roses in my back yard.
I am from my racecar and garage.
    I am from the flowers in the meadows.
        I am from my grandpa.
I am from my school.
    I am from America.
        I am from Maysville.
I am from snakes.
I am from cliff jumping with friends.
        I am from fishing with my grandpa.

And finally, the students began working on their individual poems—a process that lasted several weeks for some. The details they chose to include in this piece of writing are more than interesting and even charming—they are revealing and offer hints about how each child might read the world. Important people, places, events, and activities are dotted throughout the lines of poetry and offer possible topics for whole group, small group, and one-on-one conversations. Each writer was finding a starting point for voicing various experiences and beliefs as she located importance and value in her life. Such voicing, over time in the language classroom, would be encouraged, honed, and even challenged and nudged forward. This voicing grounded the students in their own lived experiences as they began to more closely read, understand, and question the world in which they live.

■ Writing and Living in Class Borderlands

Like Gloria Anzaldua (1999), the children in this study were living in the borderlands—the in-between spaces of their working-poor homes and their institutional existence. Anzaldua views this state of borderland living as the reason that "poets write and artists create" (95). This complex experience of living across and between cultures creates unrest for Anzaldua and pushes her to write and think—and write some more. Her writing offers her a refuge not only from the anxiety of life, but also a place to express herself, her understandings of life that differ so much from the dominant culture around her. Anzaldua's writing identity powerfully emerges in the following:

> To write, to be a writer, I have to trust and believe in myself as a speaker, as a voice for the images. I have to believe that I can communicate with images and words and that I can do it well. A lack of belief in my creative self is a lack of belief in my total self and vice versa—I cannot separate my writing from any part of my life. It is all one. (95)

This is what I imagine can happen for the girls in this study as they dig into their experiences and think about where they are *from*. Their belief in their creative selves as poets will feed their belief in their whole selves and vice versa. Just as writing and living go hand-in-hand in the work of Freire and Macedo (1987), I want living and writing to go hand-in-hand for children in my classroom. The poem they wrote on the first day of second grade is just the beginning of such a journey as they come to question and know themselves better while I simultaneously learn from details of their lives. Through such personal writing, I can attempt to walk in the shoes of the students, look at the world through their eyes, and avoid the pitfall so many students and teachers experience, as Lori put it:

> they're thinkin', screw that—you don't know *shit* about my life how are you *tell*in' me that this is how it is, *you* ain't in my life. Come walk a day in my shoes and you'll see. You give that child an opportunity to *let* you walk in their shoes *through* school through *writing*. And it'll be different.

Writing from lives is the critical beginning to making it—the schooling experience—different.

I Am From

By Cadence

I am from Ohio and I am from New York.

I am from presents.
   I am from cooking.
      I am from walking with my mom . . .
I am from going shopping for new clothes.

I am from Alabama.

I am from reading.
      I am from writing.

I am from my mom and my mom's friends.
   I am from my sisters.
I am from my cats.
I am from the birds.
I am from the crickets.
I am from the snakes in my back yard.

I am from people yelling . . .
I am from my mom's friends' kids crying.

I am from me sleeping.

Throughout each of the poems written by the second graders were themes of parents, cousins, grandparents, kids, noises, animals, recreation, and everyday events. Such writing work in the language classroom, however, is just the beginning and should leave us with more questions than answers. For example, is Cadence comforted by the yelling or does she perceive it as threatening? Who are her mom's friends and what relationship does Cadence have with their children? What are Cadence's connections to New York, Ohio, Alabama? A writing engagement such as this is an initial step into something much larger and more critically focused that will be grounded in a teacher's research of the child, her family, her community, where she is *from*. Beginning with these simplistic notions of where she or he is from, however, a student can begin to feel more comfortable bringing her life into classroom discussions, interpretations of literature, and into her daily writing—all three areas to which I paid close attention, listening for opportunities to scaffold understandings, challenge beliefs, and nudge toward the construction of hybrid identities that incorporate home and emerging academic identities. Such hybrid identities could promote academic success while allowing each girl to hold tight to those home and community identities formed within intimate relations. This developing hybrid consciousness, when embraced, creates a flexible, malleable young student who has many more possibilities than someone who merely embraces a single cultural identity (Anzaldua 1999; Delpit 1995). After providing this peek into my history, the classroom literacy space, and some writing by the students, we will now travel into the larger community called St. Francis.

■ Notes

1   From August through November I was the long-term substitute for this second grade classroom. Most of the students had been together in the first grade classroom I was studying.

2   I use both working-class and poor similarly in this book to make clear that children and families from outside mainstream middle-class, upper middle-class, or affluent classes are too often stigmatized in school and society. In addition to this, some people may consider the girls' families in this book to be "working-class" because they are indeed working, but they are also living below the federal poverty line and struggling to make ends meet, making them "poor" or "working-poor." Moving between working-class, working-poor, and poor in this book helps to complicate any fixed notion of how we categorize people based on class.

3   Write alouds are demonstrations of writing that are accompanied by the speaking of the author's words that are being written, as well as her or his thoughts about the decisions she or he is making regarding the writing itself.

Where Are Our Students From?

A Look into St. Francis

2

Many literacy educators are avid readers who voraciously consume stories in the minutes before children enter the classroom, during bus or train rides to and from work, over coffee in the morning, or within those precious moments between stretching out in bed and the deep, heavy breathing signaling much-needed sleep at night. The nooks and crannies that consist of our free time often open up worlds that we hadn't considered before, worlds that teach us something about the human spirit, about love, desperation, discrimination, and desire, about hate, motivation, segregation, and society. We pour over our reading selections and imagine if it had been us what would we have done, what might have been different, and how an experience would have made us feel. These sustained and concentrated interactions with worlds that differ from our own become our teachers of sensitivity, perspective, power, and empathy. However, reading pieces that have been carefully crafted for the purpose of having an impact on a reader need not be our only education into other worlds, for we are faced with such opportunity for learning each day; novels and persuasive essays in the form of our students, their families, and the communities from where they come become the reading materials for learning about the world more broadly. If we would perceive students and families as our teachers who help us to understand the particularities of their lives, predicaments, achievements, then we would move one step closer to resolving what Lisa Delpit calls "the monumental problems we face in providing a quality education for poor children and children of color [through opening] ourselves to learn from others with whom we may share little understanding" (1995, 131). In other words, to be good teachers, we had better be good learners. Throughout this chapter there will be excerpts from classroom interactions, descriptions of St. Francis and some of the residents, and some historical information to consider as an important part of the context within which this teaching and learning work occurred.

■ What Is Poor? A Literature-Based Discussion

"So what *is* poor?" I asked the class, pausing to consider the themes in *The Hundred Dresses* by Eleanor Estes (1944, 1974).

"You don't got the food," suggested Deandrew from the back of our group.

"No money," said another student.

Then others followed, "No lunch."

"No clothes."

"No shoes."

"No house."

"No bath."

"No friends."

"No socks."

Madeline, a robust brunette girl in the front (who often commented about my jewelry) added, "No earrings and no tongue rings."

Attempting to move the abstract conversation about economic inequity to a more concrete context, I added, "Put your finger here (on your chin) if you know someone who is poor," knowing that each of them were likely to respond. The topic itself is not one that is ignored in family and community conversations, it's the public conversation that is more challenging in the larger society.

Almost every student placed a finger on his or her chin.

"Does anyone in here think that they are poor?" I asked.

"Who?" Asks Cadence, a wide-eyed suntanned girl near the middle of the group.

"Anyone—yourself."

"Not me. I ain't poor. Not me," she said a little too quickly and loudly.

I looked at the class, "Just put your finger right here if you think you're poor."

Someone muttered, "Not me."

A different voice stated, "I'm not poor."

Johnathan, a soft-spoken blue-eyed boy quietly slipped his finger to his chin. Then he pulled it off. Then he put it back on.

Alexis, a towheaded girl looked out of the corner of her eye then turned her head to see who was looking at her. She kept her hand rested beneath her chin but never put her finger out.

Billy and Thomas, two best friends sitting near the back of our group, placed their fingers securely against their chins and looked straight ahead.

Knowing that students had talked amongst themselves about the dichotomy of "rich people" and "poor people" in the classroom and often included themselves on the poor end of the spectrum, I squatted down to share a story with them. This story, about getting my clothes from Goodwill and the Free Store when I was growing up, was about feeling ashamed at times because my family didn't have money, a story about the pride I developed as a child, the pride in my family, our fun times together, and the love we had for one another. I asked the students, "Can you be poor and be happy?" A resounding "yes" came from the small crowd, "Can you be poor and love your life with your family?" Another loud "yeah!" came from the group.

My purpose? To plant the seed that living on the poorer end of the social class spectrum does not equal unhappiness with oneself or with one's family. I had a long journey ahead of me toward cultivating these seeds in the classroom, but this was one of the initial lessons I used to insert discussions around rich and poor, social class, stereotypes, and discrimination. At this point in second grade I drew from the students' language practices of stereotyping people as either "rich" or "poor." They saw little or nothing in between, an assumption that was critically challenged later in the year (and in Chapter 11).

◼ Visual and Discursive Disconnect in St. Francis

After the previous conversation, Heather informed me, "I've seen poor people on TV before. Like when you send money." Heather's observation drives the point home: poverty is in the media as desperate charity cases, not as real characters in the lives of sitcoms, cartoons, and Disney movies. Thirteen million young people under the age of 18 were living in poverty in 2003 and 2004 (DeNavas-Walt, Proctor, and Lee 2005) and with numbers of people living in poverty increasing each year, it is likely that even more have fallen below the federal poverty level as this book goes to press. These youth are barraged daily with commercial media images and messages, many of which take a significant amount of money in which to gain access. Characters on television living in impoverished conditions are rare and often portrayed as homeless, desperate, criminal, or in the case of developing countries, starving with swollen stomachs. Children like Heather are disconnected from the messages they see and hear every day about class inequality and living poverty: they don't have swelling stomachs with flies in their eyes, but they also don't even remotely live the material lives of most children on television, in print ads, movies, videos, and even in children's literature (Allison 2002; Kohl 1996). Heather and her classmates lived in small spaces with limited food supplies and many second-hand material goods such as clothing, furniture, cooking supplies, and appliances. Some of these children had an abundance of one luxury item or another, shelves of Disney videos, or drawers of trendy clothing, or purses with imitation jewelry and makeup, or rows of video games for the latest in-home video game station.

In these small ways, children living in poverty can distance themselves from the stigma of being poor while they engage in luxurious play that they witness on television and correlate with social status. At the same time, their parents may be forced to walk long distances to work, the water and electricity may be disconnected, mattresses may be strewn on the living room floor at bedtime to conserve living space, and roaches may scatter like wildfire with the flicker of a light in the night and no money for extermination supplies or services provided by landlords. These are certainly not the experiences of most television families as they kiss goodnight and walk in their pajamas to separate bedrooms, many of which are furnished and decorated as if in an expensive showroom. Television images, advertisements, children's books, and media in general do not reflect the realities of working-poor children.

Poverty, even for children who live it, is invisible in our society; it's not discussed, it's not represented in the media, and it's not a part of the meritocratic American Life; the language that we have to consider class and poverty is dismal at best, and destructive at worst. Commercial society has normalized a *privileged* way of life, leaving those who live with few economic resources with two options: identify with being poor and be marginalized within the society or deny your connection to poverty and *still* be marginalized as others judge you based on your material life. This dichotomous notion reflects the ideas of many as they talk about poverty—either you *are* poor or you *aren't* poor. And many people have their own ideas about what being poor and living in poverty mean. Those meanings vary greatly, however, even among children living in poverty in the same community.

■ Peeking Through Windows into a Community Called St. Francis

Beautifully constructed, multifamily brownstones stand tall along tree-lined, narrow streets in St. Francis. Dogwoods bloom and pollen floats above the sidewalk, often landing on cars. Gym shoes pound the cement and a corner-store door flings open. Bikes glide down the middle of the road, brown and blonde hair flopping in the wind. A baby wobbles in her diaper and t-shirt alongside a teenage girl wearing tight-fitting jeans. A van carrying tanks of oxygen pulls up in front of a building and delivers a dose of fresh air to an elderly woman watching everything through her window.

Windows tell the stories of the urban, high-poverty, predominantly White community: some are carefully decorated with pots of flowers or pictures of loved ones; others are barely there with only shards of glass remaining after a brick was sent crashing through. Some windows display the American flag; others are open wide with fans helping to circulate air. Some windows are sheets of plywood; others display sheets made for beds. Windows are pushed open, pulled tightly closed and locked, or eliminated altogether. Hands wave out windows, heads hang out windows, young children even fall out windows to the ground below. Faith, an eight-year-old girl who lives in St. Francis, took a picture of her friend's window and wrote "My Friend's Window" to accompany her photograph:

My Friend's Window

This is a picture of my friend's window. I like it because her windows don't have black. Some do, but some don't. This is an old house because some of the black has white.

You can look out a window and look in. If a window is open you can ask if your friend can come out to play with you. You need windows because if you didn't have them, the sun wouldn't get in your house.

Faith took a photograph and wrote this accompanying story during a four-week study of metaphor. In Faith's story, windows are good for communication because people on the outside can talk to people on the inside. At any given time in St. Francis, it is appropriate to yell up to windows to greet someone, get someone's attention, or to call for someone to come outside. During my time in this community, I have yelled up and into countless windows to say hello to residents, to ask for children or one of their family members to come out and talk to me, or to see if it was a good time for me to come in for a visit. On one of the busy streets along the perimeter of St. Francis, this mode of communication created a challenge for my typically quiet voice as I cupped my hands around my mouth and used the deepest, loudest yell I could muster.

Windows are also important for people on the inside to see what's on the outside, like the elderly woman who cannot venture out into the severely polluted air of St. Francis. Callie wrote "My Home" about her home when she was

FIG. 2–1 *This is my dog Spike looking out the window of my house. He likes looking out the window because he sees great things. —Photographed and written by Callie.*

in second grade. She later photographed her dog looking out her family's kitchen window.

My Home

My home is quiet.
All I hear are cars passing by.
I see the snow.
I see the sun shining brightly out my window.
I hear feet on the sidewalk.
I see people who are sad and lonely too.
The roads are filled with cars.

Open windows offer glimpses to the "great things" and not so great things that are outside, like the sun shining brightly, and the sad and lonely people in

Callie's poem. There are many great things in and about St. Francis, but the not-so-great things are typically used as stereotypes for life within the community.

■ The Community: Complexities and Commonalities

Quite small in land area (.57 square miles), this inner-city community is complex with long-standing family disputes, social cliques, opposing views of the school, church, food pantry, and community agencies, and charged feelings about drugs, crime, prostitution, local politics, and education. I describe St. Francis as a *community* because of the familiarity of this reference as a physical space that is shared by a group or groups of people with at least something in common. The "something in common" that residents would probably agree to is anything but some warm-fuzzy concept of communal living, but instead something quite simple and straightforward: living in the same place at the same time. Everything else is up for debate in the community, with few points of agreement. St. Francis is also home to several institutions connected to the concept of community: a school, a bank, a community council, eating establishments, laundromats, corner stores, churches, a food pantry, and a homeless shelter. These institutions, however, are often the center of controversy between individual residents as well as between residents and those outsiders who operate the institutions.

"I don't like the fucking principal," Rose's grandmother told me as I sat at her kitchen table with a fan roaring at us. "He picks his favorites and forgets the rest."

"He's the best thing that happened to this place," a custodian said about the same principal of the community school. "We're lucky to have him."

Opposing views between those who were active within institutions and those who were outside of them were not uncommon, particularly regarding relations with police officers, school authorities, social service workers, and business owners. There was also a tendency for individuals to make distinctions between themselves and their perceived assumptions of other residents. Lori, mother of Cadence, made such a distinction in an informal interview:

> [W]ell, I'm probably a *lot* different from other mothers. I don't know. That's for you to know. But I feel sorry for some kids—they see parents smoking joints, drinkin'. They don't see anything wrong with it. They're raised with it in this neighborhood.

Residents of St. Francis: Difference Abounds

Unlike the static nature of lives that the term *community* might evoke, the experiences of living in St. Francis simply cannot be essentialized. Each individual not only lived in her own particular way, but she also perceived her life (and her child's life) in particular ways. The residents could not be essentialized, some had lived in St. Francis their entire lives, others had been transplanted there from various parts of the city after seeking help from the homeless shelter and other outreach agencies. Some residents began their lives in the community, moved to other areas of the city or across the country, and ended up back in St. Francis. Outside of approximately five families that had been in the community since most could remember, people tended to move fluidly in and out of St. Francis, often following family members, work opportunities, or more comfortable living arrangements. This pattern of migration between small towns, cities, and even states is one that reflects the historical migration of many of the residents in St. Francis.

Many of the families were first-, second-, third-, or even fourth-generation migrants from rural Appalachia, part of a massive migration from Appalachia to urban centers by those looking for work and a better life that occurred in the mid-to-late 1900s. My family was also part of this migration starting in the 1930s when my maternal great-grandfather made the trip from Corbin, Kentucky, to work as a mason on a landmark building in the city. After months of work, however, his wife convinced him that the place to be was "down home." Back they traveled with two young boys in tow and it wasn't until the late 1940s that my unmarried maternal grandmother made the move herself, leaving two young daughters behind while she began to build a city life. In 1958, my mother, nine years old at the time, came to the city with her grandmother and grandfather who were planning a permanent stay this time. Escaping the coal mines for good, her grandfather was employed by a local movie theatre, and her grandmother (my Granny) helped to maintain the apartment building in which they lived.

This back-and-forth migration between rural and urban spaces was not uncommon during the vast movement and remains a part of life for many country folks who have made homes in the city (Halperin 1998; Philliber and McCoy 1981; Obermiller 1996, 1999). Rose, Sarah, and Cadence had continual contact with kin in the "country," often taking road trips to visit during this study. Rose moved *from* and *back to* the Appalachian Mountain region between first and fourth grades. And Cadence's family was considering a rural move at the time of this publication.

When Whiteness Doesn't Equal Privilege

Some migrating families have been able to create and maintain a working-class lifestyle through industrial work, but many have found themselves in perpetual cycles of poverty and academic failure. Though the people in St. Francis would probably not like the term, some cultural scholars call them "Urban Appalachian." Urban Appalachians are considered an *invisible minority*, assuming that their Whiteness masks their differences from dominant culture (deMarrais 1998; Obermiller 1996; Philliber and McCoy 1981). After studying Urban Appalachians in St. Francis during the 1970s and 1980s, deMarrais writes, "Stereotypes die hard. Despite years of living in northern cities, urban Appalachian children continue to face discrimination based on stereotypic notions of who they are" (1998, 98). Stereotypes do die hard, as I was in the same community some twenty years later and still very little had changed. Stereotypes are also not limited to this particular geographic region, as Heilman (2004) has written about Ethnic Whites' marginal status outside of the area where this study took place.

As if the complexities within the community weren't challenging enough, this enclave is considered by outsiders within the larger metropolitan area to be inhabited by hillbillies and White trash who were more dangerous than the typically feared African Americans in high-poverty urban neighborhoods. Even my own family, who has a similar history and lives in a working-class community in the city, was concerned for my safety in St. Francis. My grandma squinted her eyes and pointed her finger, "You make sure you roll up your windows and lock your doors, you hear me?" Over time I eased their worries, convincing them that I had built relationships with neighborhood people, whom I'm sure would come to my aid if I ever needed it. My grandmother's trepidation was partly warranted however, for like most high-poverty urban areas in the United States, persistent drugs[1] and crime worried most St. Francis residents.

In the past, drug concerns were concentrated around marijuana, cocaine, and huffing[2] in the neighborhood. Starting in the mid 1990s, however, a swift shift occurred that has changed the landscape of drug use, drug crime, and the lives of families in St. Francis and elsewhere. Prescription drugs, especially the pain medication OxyContin (a synthetic opiate), have become increasingly popular. Once heralded the "hillbilly heroin" due to significant abuse and addiction in the Appalachian region, OxyContin has followed a similar migration pattern as its primary users and has hit urban enclaves with rural ties particularly hard. Extremely addictive and dangerous, OxyContin is known to "take over" lives and can lead to death (Tough 2001). With the recent crackdown on prescribing doctors and pharmacies, the street price of OxyContin has risen significantly to one dollar and above per milligram and the cost of fulfilling addictions of twenty milligrams to two hundred milligrams per day is pressing addicts to resort to crime, prostitution, and/or to choose a cheaper opiate—heroin.

Increase in the use of heroin propelled a rise in needle usage in the neighborhood, and needles were being found on sidewalks and in trashcans. Hepatitis C was not uncommon, and community agencies had resorted to bussing people from the neighborhood to methadone clinics more than an hour away. Still, a community activist estimated that the small neighborhood was losing approximately one person each month to overdose. People who would have never used hard drugs before were finding themselves addicted and spiraling out of control. A number of children had lost their parents, either to death or to addiction, leaving them reared solely by grandparents or other relatives. Drug addicts may blame a particular dealer, friend, societal pressures, or themselves. Families of addicts blame dealers and lack of treatment facilities and financial support available. Some community members and activists blame the pharmaceutical companies, the doctors, and the government for not making drug treatment facilities available to people with low incomes (it's nearly impossible to get a "bed" in the city). Though the blame and the solution are not concentrated and organized, the concern over a drug and crime epidemic in the community was a rare common ground, affecting nearly everyone. The girls in this study were no exception: Cadence's father was in jail under drug charges until she was in fourth grade; Alexis' father's live-in girlfriend died of a suspected overdose; Rose's brother's father died of an overdose; Faith's older brother was convicted of drug possession; Sarah's cousin was killed in a drug-related murder. All of the girls knew who was selling "weed," who was smoking it, and which kids were persuading others to join them, and they had acquired detailed knowledge and complex understandings around such issues by the time they were seven years old.

It's true that common ground was hard to find within this community, but the same is probably true of all communities. The challenges and inconsistencies within St. Francis often seemed daunting to me, a teacher/researcher/advocate, as the complex web of sometimes contradictory relations became increasingly tangled the more time I spent there. At times I felt my windows of opportunity for finding solutions to the undereducation and uneducation of poor youth in the neighborhood were being shattered by bricks of difference and discontinuity. But on occasion, a stream of light would shine through as I would discover some commonality that the residents themselves never completely articulated. These similar beliefs, desires, values, and histories will be woven throughout this text with the first being the importance of unessentializing lives in poverty and the undesired stigmas that are attached to those living with few economic resources.

Exercise 2.1 Reading Discussion

Reflect on your reading of this chapter:

● What did you connect to and why?

● What was hard for you to believe and why?

● Did you experience any epiphanies? If so, when and why?

● How does your history impact your reading of this chapter?

● What snippets of classroom stories in this chapter gave you ideas for your own literacy teaching?

The White girls and their families in this study weren't privileged by their skin color in a society that assumes Whiteness equals middle-classness, instead they were often stereotyped as outsiders of dominant White culture and assumed to be just like all of their neighbors. Essentializing St. Francis families is impossible, as demonstrated in this chapter, and jumping to conclusions about what families did at home or how they felt about school and the community would be a major mistake. Chapter 3 will continue the discussion around St. Francis, explicitly incorporating social class and poverty and literacy engagements in the classroom.

■ Notes

1   I want to point out, however, that more drugs are reportedly sold in U.S. suburbs than in inner cities (Gans 1995; Irwin 1985). More inner city, poor people are simply arrested and jailed for drug possession, trafficking, and drug-related crimes. This is likely a result of greater surveillance and stereotyping in high-poverty neighborhoods, and much of the worry of residents is because they don't have money for treatment, for good legal representation, and for bailing family members out of jail.

2   A way of intoxicating oneself through breathing the toxic fumes of various household chemicals such as spray paint, glue, etc.

3

Poverty
Living Lives on the Margins

■ A Conversation About *Overcoming*

According to federal guidelines, the girls in this study lived in poverty[1] but a girl or a family member would rarely identify herself as being poor. "We ain't rich, but we ain't poor," is a statement I heard time and again during the study. The stigma of being poor is overwhelming and can place families and children in a position of endless denial so as to not carry the burden of shame that is placed upon them by the larger society. Thus, poverty can be lived by people without their having the opportunity to voice their consciousness about poverty and class discrimination. When a class position is stigmatized so much that no one openly accepts the position, then a collective class movement is virtually impossible (Ortner as discussed in Bettie 2003). Unlike the traditional working class who have had access to unions and other collective powers, no such organized support was available for working-poor folks living in St. Francis.

Poverty is a term that is often thrown around in the United States without thinking about the *construct* of poverty, or the *effects* of poverty, or *how poverty is lived* by young children who attend school every day. Poverty is carried on the backs of children as they wear clothing that is two sizes too large, too small, and faded or stained. Poverty is located within the bellies of children as they come to school looking forward to free breakfast and lunch. Poverty, like all social class positions, is attached to the appendages of children as they use their bodies[2] to express themselves nonverbally, travel from place to place, and engage in physical interactions. Poverty is spoken by children as they use language in particular ways with particular intonations. Poverty is marked on the psyche of children as they perceive the material world, use caution in their interactions, and read the judgments around them made by others, all while denying they are poor. *These* are some of the reasons why poverty is not easily overcome. Living poverty shapes our physical, social, and psychological beings. To overcome poverty may possibly mean to overcome oneself.

The traditional picture of *overcoming* poverty is one of moving up and out of an impoverished neighborhood leaving family, friends, and familiar sights, smells, tastes, and sounds behind. Though at times it may be beneficial to put distance between oneself and sources of love, anguish, and support, most families in this study would prefer that their daughters stay "close to the nest" where they can be "safe and protected." Callie's mother suggested that her daughter could potentially be in a relationship with an abusive man and the family must be nearby to defend her. Cadence's mother understood that opportunities for employment and economic growth in the neighborhood were limited, so she hoped that her daughter could "go away for awhile—but then come back." I want the girls in this study to have the opportunity to experience life outside the neighborhood if they want, but I have also found myself growing to think and feel more like Cadence's mom—I hope they come back. Enclaves of generational poverty in America aren't going to diminish when young, talented, academically successful students only desire to get "out," taking their creative energies and potential for change with them.

Perhaps this is precisely why I didn't want these girls to overcome poverty, but instead I wanted to help them understand their experiences as central to their developing identities, and learn how their diversity could help them to be sensitive to other local and global injustices. Through this understanding I hope that the girls will grow to become—not overcome—women who have insights into living under poverty's heavy hand and who work toward the lofty goals of social justice.

◼ The Disconnect of the Global Market and Real Lives in Poverty

Commercials, sitcoms, reality television shows, cartoon networks, and televised sporting events promote and privilege idealized versions of the American Life with consumerism serving as one way to experience slices of such a life. This American Life, sometimes presented as lived in sprawling suburban homes with closets full of brand-name clothing and expensive vehicles, is peppered with *luxuries* that are presented as *necessities*: multiple telephone lines, mobile telephones, high-speed internet connections, dishwashers, riding lawnmowers, garages, power tools, and the list could go on forever. This American Life, however, is not lived by the 37 million people living in households with incomes below the poverty level in 2004 (DeNavas-Walt, Proctor, and Lee 2005). In 2001, poverty levels increased for the first time since 1993[3] with 11.7 percent of the total population considered in poverty. Those rates have continued to increase with 12.5 percent of the total population living below the poverty line in 2003 and 12.7 in 2004 (DeNavas-Walt, Proctor, and Lee 2005). Of the 36 million "poor" people in 2004, 16.9 million were White, like most of the residents in St. Francis. Official poverty levels may be even higher if all people were counted,[4] but it is not uncommon for men and women to be unemployed for years without filing a tax statement or being listed as a dependent on another person's return. Adult children living with parents or grandparents, and small families making ends meet through the informal economy[5] account for some of these people. Geographic isolation and political voicelessness render poor people invisible to the social imagination of mainstream U.S. citizens, but there are undoubtedly many who are literally nonexistent when it comes to official government counts. This failure to be "counted" through visibility by their middle-class counterparts and nationwide statistics continues a slippery slope scenario where living conditions afforded by poverty are forgotten and therefore those who live in such conditions are also forgotten in public discourse, political discourse, and social policy. Donaldo Macedo (1994) compares such geographic, economic, social, and psychological locations in the United States with the deprivation typically affiliated with developing countries:

> We are experiencing a rapid Third Worldinization of North America where inner cities resemble more and more the shantytowns of the Third World with a high level of poverty, violence, illiteracy, human exploitation, homelessness and human misery. The abandonment of our inner cities and the insidious decay of their respective infrastructures, including their schools, makes it very difficult to maintain the artificial division between the First World and the Third World. (xiii)

This scholarly acknowledgement and deep understanding about impoverished lands in North America has not trickled down to the residents of St. Francis and their children. Poverty is still somewhere else—in photographs, in developing countries, in someone else's home. The land of the United States is supposed to be classless, and the American Dream accessible to anyone who works hard and long enough. The stigma of being poor is a discriminatory one often catapulted by the global market, compulsive consumerism, and materialism in the states.

Exercise 3.1 A Privileged Life

Some of you reading this text may have the privilege of easy access to material goods and services that make your life comfortable. Consider how a privileged position helps one to negotiate life with more ease than someone without such resources.

- How do you get to work in the morning? Is transportation ever a stressful issue for you? When? Consider not having transportation (a car, money for the bus, a coworker who picks you up) and getting to work each day. If you have a car, how is it maintained? Consider deciding between paying the electric bill and getting an oil change or a tune-up.

- What do you wear to work and how does this contribute to others' perceptions of you? Consider building your wardrobe solely from the selection at a local Goodwill or thrift store. How might others' perceptions of you change? How might life be more challenging if you didn't have access to the kind of clothing "expected" for your position?

- How do you communicate with loved ones? Do you have a telephone? Email? Consider getting word to your mother or father that your child is sick and you need an emergency babysitter so you can work. No email. No phone. How might this complicate your life as you ready yourself to leave for the day? Consider walking a block with a sick child to a neighbor's home where you have used the telephone before and the neighbor doesn't answer the door. Now what?

Three simple categories, transportation, clothing, and communication, should stimulate some productive conversation around privileges that many people in the United States take for granted every single day.

- List some of privileges you enjoy each day—begin with your waking up in the morning to a home supplied with electricity and running water.

- Consider life without these privileges.

- Think about the families in your school who live without some or most of these privileges each day and describe your respect for them and their ability to negotiate life without access to resources that often make life easier.

◾ Connecting Ourselves Through Discussions Around Poverty

In November of their second grade year, I began an afterschool program for the girls in my study. One goal of mine was to sanction topics around social class, being poor, struggling to make ends meet, and the real value and knowledge gained through such experiences. I also wanted to engage the girls in conversations around poverty that penetrated the dichotomy mentioned earlier in this book: either you're poor or you're not. The children intuitively knew things were more complicated than this but it was rarely acknowledged in classroom discussions around literature and life.

After reading *Best Sandwich,* a poem by Vera B. Williams (2001) about two girls snuggling together with their teddy bear as they await their mother's nighttime arrival from work, the girls and I engaged in a discussion that built upon past conversations we had had around social class and poverty. Heather asked the group, "Are they poor?" Her question began a discussion that led to a more complicated understanding of what it means to be poor:

"Yeah," answered Joanie.

"What do you think, Heather?" I asked.

"Yeah, because they said only crackers were on the shelf. They don't have other stuff like macaroni and cheese," she responded.

"Are they poor? What do you think?" I asked the other girls.

Joanie changed her mind about her answer, "No," she said, "cuz they got money—they're workin' for money cuz their mom is at work."

"How do you know?" asked Heather, "Her mom might have a different job."

Cadence joined the discussion, "She has crackers, so they're not poor, so they can have food. Poor people don't have food."

"But that's the only thing they got—crackers," Heather still believed a lack of a *variety* of foods made them poor.

Though we came to no consensus of whether or not the girls in the poem were in fact poor, the conversation presented here is very different from the conversation around *The Hundred Dresses* that took place at the beginning of their second grade school year (Chapter 2). Here, relativity is recognized and discussed as complexities about life experiences are explored.

Being "poor" is relative. As our conversation around *Best Sandwich* continued, Heather often reminded our group that we "should be thankful for what you got," that others have less. Joanie reported that her cousin, who was also in our group, was rich. Economically speaking, however, "rich" is also a relative concept. According to federal guidelines, her cousin, Callie, also lived in poverty. If being poor is relative, then the concept of poverty must also signify relativity. This is clear to those who actually *live* poverty, but it is often much less clear to those who read, write, and talk about poverty within various political, scholarly, and social circles.

Robert Coles and Randy Testa (2001) challenged the typical physical description of poverty to pursue more social and psychological experiences through gathering excerpts from literary works about and by people who have experienced it themselves. Within this anthology Dorothy Allison writes, "I know that some things must be felt to be understood, that despair, for example, can never be adequately analyzed; it must be lived" (2001, 77). Poverty may also be a concept that can never be adequately analyzed; it must be lived to be felt, to be fully understood and to have the grounding necessary to think deeply about the implications for schools and society.

The poor are often classified as a monolithic group by nonpoor people regardless of how they came to be poor, what resources they have access to outside of government programs, the stability of their housing and food supply, their kinship networks, and their intellectual and spiritual growth outside educational institutions. Some speak empathetically about the poor, others condemn, and still others make it their life work to end economic inequalities in the United States. Heather, Cadence, and Joanie, however, didn't perceive being poor as a cut-and-dry issue. To speak about poverty, for these young girls who lived it, was to speak of relativity, of complexities, of contradictions—poor was always debatable. In the preceding conversation, Joanie believed that someone who was working certainly couldn't be poor, but Heather argued that the mother could have a different kind of job, perhaps a job that doesn't pay very well, or a job that doesn't pay at all such as helping others in the community without expecting anything in return. Both of these girls had two biological parents living at home; each had a job. The contradictions were fierce.

■ The Psyche of Poverty and Disconnect from School

The disconnect many people may experience as they view television programs grounded in affluence mirrors what they may feel as they walk into school each day. Media images may be perceived as a fantasy world, a world in which the young students can't really belong, or even think of belonging—or perhaps these images offer a way for people to live a luxurious life vicariously through the television characters' lives. Pieces of that material world, such as high-tech items (computer, cell phone, video games), stylish-looking clothes, or even a particular piece of furniture, can sometimes be gained. Acquiring these pieces is a luxury to a person struggling to pay the bills; I often shopped in second-hand stores to find that piece of clothing, furnishing, or jewelry that looked hip and paid a fraction of the price that it would have been in a department store or specialty shop. Wearing a certain kind of attire that appeared to be expensive often made me feel like I belonged—especially in school.

My lavender knee-pocketed, tapered-legged cotton pants are one example. On the right knee was a triangle with one corner pointing downward and on this triangle was a brand name (something I don't even remember now—was it Palmetto's?), but the triangle was the same size as a GUESS? triangle. My mom, being the clever, resourceful woman she was, found a discarded piece of GUESS? clothing at the thrift store, carefully removed the triangle, and meticulously stitched it to my lavender knee-pocketed, tapered-legged cotton pants. Suddenly I felt special, a simple changing of the triangles, but I was a brand new person. Everyone would see that I, too, had clothes that bore the name of the most popular line at the time: GUESS? Even with this newfound material identity, I lived with the constant fear that someone at school would recognize the illegitimacy of my clothes and confront me with the truth: I did not own an authentic pair of GUESS? brand pants. Being discovered a fake would be worse than never having had the pants, but I put myself at this risk to bask in the short-term glory of wearing would-be designer clothes.

This was one small way that I was able to become a part of the media images surrounding me. Many working-poor and working-class people go to extremes to have a slice of the All-American consumer pie, and to get a piece of it for their child is important to those who experienced marginalization in school themselves. Daisy, Rose's mother, told emotionally charged tales of the teasing, taunting, and physical abuse she faced at school because she didn't have the kind of clothes the "popular kids" had. Daisy, Rose's father, and Rose's grandmother worked hard to give Rose what they perceived she needed to fit in with the kids at school: Mary-Kate and Ashley outfits from Kmart, dress shoes with sparkles and glitter, leopard-print purse and other accessories, and dark blonde hair from a box purchased at a local drugstore. "Fitting in," or meeting the perceived requirements of mainstream America, was clearly something Rose's family thought much about as they tried to equip her with the material goods and physical attributes advertised on television and elsewhere.

Rose wasn't the only one who had a loving and doting family attempting to get a piece of the All-American pie for her; her story conjures images of all the girls in this study. I think of Cadence's second-hand Tommy Hilfiger pants that were at least two sizes too large, cuffed four times and held up by a belt. Alexis carried a trendy plastic purse with dangling earrings, a necklace, a ring, and bright pink lipstick. Callie boasted about her platform denim gym shoes with silver glitter and talked about her "Mary-Kate and Ashley" videos at home. Heather adorned flare-legged silver-studded jeans and had shelves of Disney videos. Faith wore a flashy jogging suit with the name of a popular basketball team embroidered on the front. There is no doubt that the parents who bought these items either worked extra hours to do so or lived without something else in their life for the short-term (e.g., Wilkerson 2005) in sacrifice. Aunts, uncles, grandmas, or older cousins also splurged on these material goods so their loved ones wouldn't be ridiculed or shamed because of their clothing or lack of other status goods.

Money Can't Buy a Discourse[6]

Fitting in socially with classmates at school is one thing, but fitting in as an academic success in school is a bit different—you can't find the language of schooling at the local free store or at the thrift shop, work extra hours to buy it at a department store, or get your aunt to buy it for you. You can't even trade a service such as fixing a car for someone who has a Discourse you want. And no matter how many times your parents tell you to "do good" in school, you're not quite equipped to do so: Money can't buy a new Discourse. A luxury item may help a young girl feel like she belongs with her peers in school and within the larger consuming society, but material goods alone don't significantly change language, relations, beliefs, or identities. This fact is quickly realized when students and families interface with teachers and administrators in schools.

Far different from media images and fantasies of luxurious lives portrayed on television, in films, and in magazines, teachers and principals are *real* people who live *real* lives in material conditions that most of the girls and families in this study could only dream of. A lesson that is implicitly absorbed is that social class difference is typically accompanied by judgment and relentless comparison to the standards of the people whom children and families find working in schools.

Exercise 3.2 Getting to Know a Community: Teacher-Researchers

Getting to know the community in which you work is imperative for a more in-depth understanding of the social and cultural lives your students and their families live. As presented in this chapter, children experience different realities even within one very small, seemingly homogeneous neighborhood. Once we know a community well we can better discuss the resources of the community (or the "funds of knowledge" as in Moll 1999) as well as potential challenges in positive, productive ways and know better how to build real bridges between home and school. Use or adapt the framework in the table to conduct a ministudy through observations, interviews, informal discussions, photography, and document research through newspapers, published books, and publications within the community. Group work around this topic would not only engage more people in important ways, but it will increase the probability that these considerations will become part of the language practices of your teaching team, grade level, school, and/or district.

Geography	People	Institutions	Activity/ Recreation	Activity/ Work
Investigate the physical space of the community and how it is divided.	Get to know and describe various families in the community. Investigate any tensions between family or friendship groups.	What are the physical institutions in the community (bank, school, health, community outreach, long- standing stores, diners, bars). Which are government-run? Volunteer-run? Independently run?	What do families/individuals do for recreation?	Describe adult work (paid work, domestic work, child-rearing work, bartering work, etc.).
Describe the relationship between particular people and the physical space.	What informal structures are in place to support family members, extended family, and neighbors?	Where do different residents feel most welcome and comfortable? Why? Where do residents feel least comfortable? Why?	Describe the relationship between recreation and family, how do they shape one another?	Get to know and describe child work (chores, expectations, sibling care, paid work).

Why were families drawn (or pushed) to this physical place?	What roles do children take on in families and in the community?	Describe relations between community members and people representing different institutions (social workers, teachers, police officers, loan officers, etc.).	Describe the connection between recreation and economic resources, how do they shape one another?	Where do people go to work and how do they get there?
How and when did various families arrive in this place? Describe any tension.	What do families want for their children? Do they hope they move away? Stay nearby? Describe any tension.	Are there "insiders," meaning community people, work-ing in various institutions? If so, how does this impact the lives of these residents?	Describe patterns of recreation (children and families)— daily, weekly, monthly, by season, and annually.	How is "work" understood and what do adults want for their children in terms of "work" for their future? Describe any tension.

Consider the following questions in relation to the ministudy findings:

- What are implications for our school vision?

- What are implications for classroom practice?

- What are implications for institutional structures we have in place?

- How can we use this information to forge relationships with families and community?

- How can we more productively position ourselves in the community?

- In what ways can we continue this research since the families we serve will change?

- In what ways can we mentor new educators to be a part of this community? In other words, how can we make this kind of activity a systematic part of our work?

■ Class, Discourse, and Schooling

bell hooks (2000) wrote about her experiences in school as a young girl from working-class roots in the segregated rural South, an experience peppered with lessons about social class that were implicitly understood. The beginning of hooks' class consciousness seems to have rooted in some of her earliest memories of school:

> Even as we sat next to the children of black doctors, lawyers, and undertakers in our segregated schoolrooms, no one talked about class. When those children were treated better, we thought it was because they were prettier, smarter, and just knew the right way to act. Our mother was obsessed with teaching us how to do things right, teaching us manners and bourgeois decorum. Yet she had not been around enough middle-class black people to know what to do. (21)

Through this narrative we can read her confusion, her anxiety as she looked to classmates that were treated better simply because of their class status. Though she had not yet developed a critical lens on class, hooks began to develop a consciousness as she recognized early in life that certain attributes or characteristics were deemed more valuable than others in the classroom. We can also envision her mother repeatedly telling hooks to act right and to mind her manners, but never having the experience herself to model these behaviors for her daughter. The mother wanted hooks to perform a Discourse respected at school, but she was unable to immerse her in, or teach her the Discourse herself. Similar tensions arose time and again between the daughters and mothers of this study. The mothers urged their daughters to take a different path than they had taken, but equipping the girls with ways of using language and being in the world that were different from theirs is easier said than done, as we will see in Chapter 8.

Many social class lessons are learned implicitly, passed on from generation to generation, from teacher to student, through peer groups, and through media. The lessons may be hardest in school, however, due to some of the reasons that are discussed in this chapter. Over time, students become aware of social class discrimination and may respond in resistant, subordinate, or inconsistent ways. Some of these responses could include dropping out of school, skipping school, overtly and aggressively resisting school authorities, performing identities in school to reflect the dominant norm, and any combination of these even if they contradict one another. Confusion abounds and many voices are silenced. This silencing phenomenon doesn't only happen in and through schools, but it is also at work in families as a defense mechanism in response to institutions that reflect dominant cultural values. This silencing is also at work in the society at large, where social class and class discrimination are ignored almost entirely.

In Chapter 4 we learn valuable lessons from children who silence their own experiences in the context of literacy events in the classroom. Some children do this to appear more "normal" by dominant society standards, and others silence themselves in response to peers who have already bought into what is and isn't normal according to their perceptions of teachers' beliefs. The result of this self-surveillance is counterproductive and can have devastating effects as students feel less and less like they belong in school and become more and more likely to disengage psychologically, socially, cognitively, and physically.

▓ Notes

1   Approximately 93.5 percent of students attending Bruger Elementary School received free lunch; 4.1 percent received lunch at a reduced rate. Fifty-six percent of all families in St. Francis lived below the federal poverty level with the official unemployment rate 16 percent and joblessness at 50 percent (Maloney and Auffrey 2004).

2   Much like Bourdieu's concept of *habitus*.

3   Tony Pugh (2002) "Poverty Levels Up for the First Time Since 1993" for Knight-Ridder Newspapers.

4   Over 2 million people in the U.S. jails and prisons are not counted in these statistics, nor are the estimated 12 million undocumented immigrants living in the United States (Bowman 2006).

5   See Rhoda Halperin's *Practicing Community*, for a discussion of the informal economy in working-class communities.

6   Discourse is used here as an identity that includes language practices, interaction styles, dress, walk, and so on that helps one to be recognized as a part of a specific group. A middle-class mainstream Discourse, for example, is one that is traditionally valued in schools and classrooms where students are expected to walk, talk, behave, dress, and interact in ways that reflect the Discourse (Gee 1996).

4

Taboo No More
Validating Lives on the Margins

◼ Never Play with a Bully: A First Grade Read-Aloud

Cadence sits on the floor with the rest of her classmates preparing to listen to Ms. Lockhart's[1] read-aloud. Cadence's gray cotton-weave shirt is inside out and the legs of her blue jeans creep up her shins revealing colored socks and untied, scuffed gym shoes. Ms. Lockhart begins to read a story aloud and the students attend closely learning about a character considered to be a bully. The moral of the story is to *not* be a bully and before the end of the book Ms. Lockhart asks the students, "Do any of you know someone who is a bully?" The students respond with bubbling enthusiasm mentioning this name and that name of bullies on the playground and in their neighborhood. Cadence raises her hand, "My dad is a bully." Ms. Lockhart looks at Cadence, and quietly moves on to the next person. Cadence's eyes dart down to the floor and she scoots herself back about six inches. As Ms. Lockhart finishes the book, Cadence twists her jersey-knit gray sleeve around her hand, biting on it until it is soaked through. After finishing the book Ms. Lockhart asks the class, "Do we ever want to play with bullies?" In unison, the first graders answer their teacher: "Noooooooooo." Cadence sits quietly staring at the floor.

Exercise 4.1 From Where Do You Read?

How do you "read" this classroom vignette?

● Do you read this scenario differently as a female, male, teacher, parent, child, working-class person, affluent person, administrator?

- Does your history, race, religion, sexuality impact your reading of this scenario?

- What values are privileged, or assumed to be normal, within your readings?

- Who might be offended or demeaned by your readings?

■ Critical Literacy and Multiple Perspectives

An imperative part of engaging in critical literacies is to have the ability to read from multiple perspectives and evaluate various perspectives in terms of social critique, power, discrimination, and oppression (e.g., Kempe 1993). Before reading from multiple perspectives, however, we must understand our own cultural locations and how those locations impact *our* perspectives. For example, because I was raised White, female, and working-poor has much to do with how I make sense of the world around me. Other particular locations that I embody include:

- Married
- Heterosexual
- Spiritual
- Physically mobile
- Mentally and emotionally stable
- Academic researcher
- Mother
- Daughter
- Sister
- Aunt
- Sister-in-law
- English speaker
- Speaker of at least two dialects in English

My list could go on and on and so could yours. Your list, like mine, will set you up to have certain kinds of readings of students and their literacy engagements in the classroom. The knowledge we have of the child and her family, for example, will change our readings and the value we place on their lives. The more we consider multiple perspectives the better equipped we will be to consider questions[2] central to critical literacy:

- What kind of world is normal or "privileged" in this text[3]?

- Who and what is not represented in this text?

- Whose interest does this text serve?

- In what ways can this text be challenged?

- How is power exercised in this text?

- Who is marginalized—or seemingly without power—in this text?

As I "read" Cadence's scenario and the conversation around bullying, I consider these questions that help me move toward a perspective that privileges experiences that are not typically represented in schools: those of working-class and poor children and families.

■ A Conflict of Class-Specific Values

Ms. Lockhart is engaged in a discursive, or language, practice that signifies her White, middle-class, teacher identity as she presents a lesson to this group of children about bullying. This is a lesson that may occur in many classrooms, by many well-meaning teachers like Ms. Lockhart. Her belief, intertwined with her social class positioning, is that her job is to teach these children how to behave in a way that reflects the dominant values within our society; those of the White middle class. The privileging of the values of the middle class during literacy education is problematic however, as students are placed in a position of choosing whether or not to judge their own family and community members from the perspective of their teacher and the school. This is one process in which the *oppressed* become the *oppressors*, a phenomenon articulately described in the work of Paulo Freire (1970).

Cadence attempted to enter an academic practice of responding to literature and to her teacher when she said "My dad is a bully." Cadence took the leap of faith by merging her two worlds: a girl in the "real world" and a girl in a classroom. When Ms. Lockhart responded with silence and moved on to another child, Cadence's voiced experience representing a part of her world was silenced, marginalized in the space of the classroom. At that moment Cadence could recognize that Ms. Lockhart's values (and those privileged at school) did not necessarily include hearing her lived reality. Cadence's life connections to literature are not valued and her experiences are not validated.

This is the same disconnect that students from poor and working-class families have felt for generations in educational institutions (Finn 1999; hooks 1994, 1996, 2000b; Reay 1998; Rist 2000; Walkerdine 1998; Walkerdine et al. 2001). Students often feel they must "be somebody else" (Walkerdine 1998) as they enter an educational institution and several of Ms. Lockhart's young first graders from St. Francis had already learned this lesson well by the time she read this book to them. Only two weeks after the read-aloud of *Tyrone and the Swamp Gang* when every student said they would never play with bullies, a small group of students began talking about fighting and bullying. Following a discussion about family members and classmates who fight, one student said, "It ain't fair to call somebody a bully."

"Are you a bully sometimes?" I asked.

"Yeah."

This conversation was not sanctioned and occurred in the back of the room during reading workshop, far from the regular classroom teacher. As a researcher in the classroom, I happened to be nearby and pulled myself closer to eavesdrop. When the students noticed I was listening and not reprimanding them for the fighting conversation they began to include me. These very young children—six and seven years of age—had already learned to be somebody else when they entered school and engaged in literacy activities with people who have different values and lives than they. Cadence was just beginning to learn this hard lesson—she was still trying to merge her two class-specific worlds of home and school.

■ The Story Behind "My Dad Is a Bully"

I had been a teacher-researcher in Cadence's classroom since the first day of first grade, learning a lot about Cadence through our academic conferences (e.g., writing/reading workshop, math) and through our informal chats before school, in the halls, and in the cafeteria. When she said, "My dad is a bully," I thought, "Which dad is she talking about?" Her biological father, whom she called dad, was in jail under drug charges, and her mom had a boyfriend whom Cadence also referred to as "dad," but not consistently. In a writing conference, Cadence discussed her dad and her "stepdad."

CADENCE: Because now we can't see him and he can't see us. And it's not fair cuz our stepdad is mean to us and our real dad is just nice. Cuz when they make a mess, they tell us to clean it up.

STEPHANIE: Who's they?

CADENCE: My stepdad.

STEPHANIE: What about your mom?

CADENCE: She gets into a fight with my stepdad, with her boyfriend, because he told us that we have to move out when we're eighteen and my mom got mad and if my real dad got out of jail he's gonna leave us.

STEPHANIE: Who's gonna leave you?

CADENCE: My mom's boyfriend.

STEPHANIE: Oh, if your real dad is back at home?

CADENCE: Uh-huh.

Cadence connected the actions of the bully in the story to her experiences with her stepdad. He told people what to do and was the boss around the house when it came to Cadence and her sisters and perhaps her mother. However, I want to pursue the possibility that Cadence was *also* connecting the bully identity in this story to herself and others in her classroom. Perhaps for Cadence, offering her stepdad as a bully was safer than admitting to the teacher that she and/or her classmates were bullies.

■ Who's a Bully?

It was well known and documented in this school that a lot of fighting took place in the halls, on the playground, and outside school, and Cadence and her first grade classmates were no exceptions. Fighting was a daily occurrence and often a mode of survival or a call for respect in the neighborhood, making it a topic that came up quite often during conversations around literature. On an early spring day during the same first grade year Ms. Lockhart was reading books about heroes:

"How can you be someone's hero?" she asked the class.

"You can fight for them," called out one of the boys.

"Not fight, well you can fight for someone without having a fist fight," Ms. Lockhart answered.

Though Ms. Lockhart was aware of the school's problem with fighting, she might not have understood how this played out in the lives of her students. In an interview, Cadence revealed how fighting played a part in her life and in her future aspirations:

CADENCE: I'm gonna be a fighter when I grow up.

STEPHANIE: You're gonna be a fighter?

CADENCE: Yeah.

STEPHANIE: So, who you gonna fight?

CADENCE: Um, I don't know.

STEPHANIE: Like, do you know people who are fighters?

CADENCE: Yeah.

STEPHANIE: Who?

CADENCE: My sisters, my cousins, my aunt, my friends, and um, I have . . . um . . . and I am.

STEPHANIE: And you are?

CADENCE: Uh-huh.

STEPHANIE: When do you fight?

CADENCE: Uh, I fight my sisters, they be mean to me. And, um . . . and, my uncle is a fighter.

STEPHANIE: Your uncle is a fighter? So what does your uncle do?

CADENCE: He fights on the weekends when he doesn't work, he's in karate.

(Conversation continues about uncle fighting—it's hard for me to tell if Cadence is talking about sparring in the karate class, or if she is talking about street fighting, or bar fighting, or fighting in the home. Conversation turns to how sisters fight for Cadence. "They fight for me.")

STEPHANIE: Do they beat up people in the karate class or in other places?

CADENCE: Like outside, the house, or like it can be done at the park. These two boys was arguing over a pop. Then they started arguing and got into a fight and everyone down at the park was watching. And they started fighting and everyone was screaming and it was giving me a headache

STEPHANIE: What were you feeling like?

CADENCE: I was feeling like I was about to shout why? So I can make them stop if I screamed out loud.

STEPHANIE: Did it scare you?

CADENCE: Uh-huh—cuz my sister was fighting.

STEPHANIE: At the same time?

CADENCE: Yeah.

According to Cadence, fighting is a part of life and perhaps people in her family, including herself, could be considered bullies in the eyes of Ms. Lockhart. Cadence hinted at her wondering of why fighting was such a way of life, but this didn't interfere with her determination to be a fighter when she grows up.

So, who's the bully? From Ms. Lockhart's perspective, a bully is one who acts in the ways that the main character in the book acts: bossing people around and being aggressive. This definition of a bully is extended as she opened up the conversation to the students and they talk about people pushing and fighting on the playground, behaviors easily incorporated into Ms. Lockhart's definition of a bully. From this perspective, any of the children and many of their family members could be considered a bully; at one time or another almost all of them had physically fought with someone to solve a problem. From the perspective of at least one child in the classroom, however, "It ain't fair to call somebody a bully." Perhaps this view is one that reflects the writing of Gans (1995) as he explores the various reasons people living in poverty may act in ways that seem "irresponsible" to the mainstream society—survival is top priority.

Exercise 4.2 Rethinking Narrow Definitions of Character That Privilege Middle-Class and Upper Middle-Class Lives

---

Consider the following questions:

- How can multiple perspectives be brought into lessons such as this one on bullying?

- How can we create spaces where students not only attempt to merge their two worlds of home and school, but are rewarded and validated when they do so?

- Hindsight is 20/20. If you realized this class conflict occurred in your classroom, what could you do the following day to attempt resolve?

■ Reading Cadence, Writing Workshop, and Jail

In September of first grade, Cadence wrote and talked about her dad in jail and often fantasized about his release and the reunion they would have, but in April of first grade, Cadence informed me she had stopped writing about her dad.

"Because then everybody's gonna know and they're gonna know why he's in jail and I didn't want them to know."

"You didn't want them to know?" I asked.

"No. I think they will make fun of me. Like Octavia. Octavia's making fun of me."

"What did Octavia say?"

"He was saying that 'your dad's in jail' and then he started laughing."

"And what did you say back to him?"

"I didn't say anything. I didn't wanna get in truvle."

"What *would* you have said back to him?" I probed.

"I wanted to say, 'stop making fun of me!'"

Hearing this about Octavia surprised me. I was sure that he knew people who were in jail, but I didn't realize that *his* dad was in jail until second grade when I was the students' full-time teacher/researcher for eleven weeks. Aiming to validate the outside-of-school lives of the students, I listened intently to their comments and discussions and foregrounded topics that had been ignored during their first grade year. *Jail* was one of those topics.

On a warm September morning in second grade, I was preparing the students that two girls in the class, Joanie and Callie, had lost their grandma and they would be coming in after the funeral that same morning. Our morning meeting turned to a discussion about death and dying and then a student, Brian, unknowingly invited the topic of jail when he mentioned his mother.

"My real mom died because she got real sick." Brian's mom died of an overdose when he was very young, and he lived with his grandma and grandpa because his biological father was in jail. Many of the children knew Brian's circumstance, and perhaps this is why Baker felt comfortable immediately adding his comment, "and my dad's in jail."

Derek, another boy in the classroom who lived near Brian said, "Brian's daddy's in jail too."

"I knew that," said Baker.

Suddenly our morning meeting circle was like popcorn popping with voices coming from around the circumference reporting who was in jail.

"My stepdaddy's in jail," said Derek.

"My dad's in jail," Cadence added.

Sandra chimed in, "My mom was in jail."

Octavia snapped, "MY dad's in jail," turned his body and looked away.

"Raise your hand if you just said your dad or stepdad is in jail," I said to the class.

"My uncle's in jail," Sandra said as she raised her hand.

I watched the hands go up, surprised by the sheer number. I knew about most of the students whose fathers were in jail but not all, like Octavia. He was the one who made fun of Cadence in first grade for having a father in jail, and his teasing resulted in Cadence's reluctance to talk or write about her dad.

Seven of the eighteen students had a father or stepfather who was in jail at the time and Sandra's mother had been recently released. Nearly 50 percent of these children knew the topic of jail intimately and if I had asked the question, "Who knows someone in jail?"' chances are that even more children would have raised their hands. The topic of jail, one that is not typically addressed in primary-aged classrooms, was a concept that was woven throughout the lives of the children who were sitting around the circle with me.

■ Sanctioning "Jail"

Knowing that Cadence had been conflicted regarding writing about her dad, I decided to use her as an example to encourage others to write about their experiences with jail, if they chose, during writing workshop. I continued our morning meeting:

"You know what you could do—and I know Cadence did this sometimes last year—you could write about it." I began.

"I don't want to!" said Octavia, shaking his head back and forth vigorously.

"You don't have to if you don't want to, Octavia."

"Do what?" asked Derek.

"Write about your dad or stepdad being in jail." I answered.

Derek shook his head no and looked down, scratching his leg.

"Do you ever think about it?" I asked.

Derek nodded his head yes.

"Then why don't you want to write about it?"

"Cuz. I feel like drawing a picture." Derek mumbled.

"Draw a picture, then. Artists do that all the time. Something makes them feel angry or sad inside, then they draw a picture or write to help them take care of their feelings. And you know what? I know people in my family who have been in jail. I have an uncle who is in jail right now, and I don't get to see him."

Students who had been talking amongst themselves sat up tall and listened intently, they were surprised that I knew someone in jail. "And you know, in writing workshop you can write about anything you want."

For a discussion that lasted less than three minutes, it was quite powerful; sanctioning this topic that was embedded in their lives had long-lasting effects.

The next week Cadence published the following story about her dad:

> I look at the stars at night because it reminds me of my dad. I cannot see my dad until fifteen years are over. I cannot wait until I can see my dad. I love my dad so much that I can't wait until I see him again. He is in jail. He looks at the stars. I wonder if he is looking at the stars and thinking of me.

In October, Octavia (who had ridiculed Cadence in first grade) wrote the following story:

> I remember when my dad was in jail for shooting people because they was trying to shoot him. He was in New York. I was there. They shot the glass and almost shot me. I was scared.

Other students wrote about family members in jail, and some never wrote a word on the topic. The important part here is that I, the authority figure in the classroom, foregrounded a topic that had been taboo in the students' previous classroom and used it as a way to validate home lives. Cadence's and

Octavia's stories are highlighted in this chapter because of their history around this topic in first grade. Octavia's father was in jail during first grade too, but he had already learned the tough lesson that the values privileged in school do not necessarily include having a family member incarcerated. He had learned to be somebody else, and had internalized the values he perceived the school authorities to have, as he laughed at Cadence for being in the same predicament as himself without whispering a word about his own situation.

This all changed when the topic was sanctioned in second grade and Octavia realized he wouldn't be shamed when he shared his story about his father. Cadence no longer felt threatened either, and she continued to develop as a writer, oftentimes writing about her life.

▓ Teachers Facing Choices

Teachers and researchers have choices to make when we hear these stories: we can ignore them, judge them from one perspective, or we can hear and sanction them. I argue for sanctioning these topics and valuing many ways of living. White (2001) writes of a girl in her classroom living in poverty:

> If we silence Janice's story, we do it to benefit ourselves, the privileged and the powerful, because we don't have to change what we can't see. We have to look hard and see. (198)

I couldn't agree more with White. We are often afraid of what we might hear, afraid of the guilt we may feel, the sadness we may experience, or the hopelessness that may overcome us. But we must stop protecting ourselves because protecting ourselves in this way is hurting children as they begin to disconnect from school. The silencing of children's stories makes their lives seem worthless. No teacher says this explicitly, but perceptive students *read* teachers well, just as we read students.

Octavia and Cadence experienced a silencing of their experiences outside of school that didn't match the experiences of their teacher. Through this silencing, Octavia read that his experience of having a father in jail was not normal or valued, thus he took on more mainstream values and ridiculed Cadence for having similar experiences as he did. Cadence took a different approach—she shut down. Each of these coping strategies, however, is detrimental to the development of Cadence and Octavia as students, people, and future participants in a democracy. When we silence children's experiences we are shutting off the growth of our society and the real possibility for critical consciousness and social change.

In Chapter 5 we will explore the dangers of silencing experiences in poverty as well as discussions around social class that should be a part of our society's repertoire for understanding inequity, discrimination, and oppression. Much like the ways in which race, gender, religion, sexuality, and language have entered popular discourses, we need to make spaces for talk around class.

■ Notes

1 Ms. Lockhart was the regular classroom teacher in first grade where I was a participant-observer and many times a co-teacher.

2 This short list of questions is adapted from various sources including Comber (1998) and Kempe (1993).

3 *Text* is considered to include spoken or written words as well as visual images.

Silence Louder Than Drums

Personal and Public Consequences

5

In May of 2005 the *New York Times* began a three-week series of articles on social class in the United States, a concept worthy of reporting because, in the reporters' words, it is "a dimension of the national experience that tends to go unexamined if acknowledged at all" (Scott and Leonhardt 2005). A heaviness collected on my chest as I read that introductory article titled "Shadowy Lines that Still Divide" and whispered to myself, "Finally. Someone is talking about class in nuanced and productive ways." During those three weeks I rushed to the door each morning before changing out of my pajamas and thumbed through the bundle of newsprint hoping to find another piece in the series. Having borrowed the words of Sherry Ortner describing the United States as "discursively disabled" when it comes to social class, I had already given considerable thought to the silent but powerful role that social class plays in our society, and this series of articles published in one of the nation's most popular newspapers had me hoping that in some small way the silence could be broken.

Later that summer the silence was breeched again as Hurricane Katrina let loose on the Gulf Coast, pushing the levees in New Orleans to the breaking point, allowing contaminated flood waters to overtake the most impoverished neighborhoods of a city and wash out many lives that had been struggling to survive race- and class-based discrimination. For days and weeks following Hurricane Katrina and the devastation that unfolded in newspapers and on radio and television, I tossed and turned at night thinking of the faces I had seen, the children so helpless and innocent, and their families going to extraordinary measures to try and save them. Relatives deciding who would climb to the attic to be with the children and who would remain on the ground level and fight the rising waters with all they had left were my heroes—heroes who reminded me of my own family members, my uncles, aunts, cousins, grandparents, siblings. Dead bodies lying in the streets near the New Orleans Convention Center carefully covered by loved ones and sometimes by strangers doing what they could to protect the dignity of those who could not make it one more minute in the unforgiving heat without water or food or hope. These images and their accompanying stories nearly paralyzed me throughout the crisis; I was rendered speechless and immobile by sadness, sympathy, outrage, and imagined vengeance. The predominant blackness of the faces and bodies screamed to me that something had gone seriously wrong with the evacuation plans, that racial inequity was at play in this crisis, and that social class discrimination was the anchor that held those bodies in the city's center when their more affluent counterparts had evacuated. Perhaps *now* that we have witnessed such class inequity with our own eyes and heard the stories with our own ears and felt the experiences with heavy hearts, quivering chins, and tear-drenched cheeks we can begin asking ourselves why the social class divide is so great and wide in the richest nation on the globe. I was temporarily paralyzed but hopeful that poverty and social class-based discriminatory practices would enter political and social discourses and perhaps even be catapulted into social policy that might seriously combat the causes and effects of poverty. Like a number of folks working to better understand such inequality, for me "Hurricane Katrina kicked up the hope that the United States might try once again to seriously address the problem of poverty" (Keyssar 2005, B6).

Soon after the Armageddon-like events however, popular discourse around the poverty of those most punished by nature included their "thug"-ness; reports (now known to have been exaggerated) of vandalism, robberies, rapes, and gun fights pervaded, continuing a long discursive tradition in our country to cast those who are poor in a light of unworthiness, deserving of the mistreatment they receive. Ignorant classist remarks about why residents had not evacuated when warned ignore the social, political, and economic realities of life without easy access to transportation to get out of the city and without money for lodging outside the city for an unknown period of time. Savings accounts and credit cards probably served middle-class New Orleaneans well in their escape, but working-class and poor folks tend not to have such luxurious safety nets. Tens of thousands sought protection and security for themselves and their families in the Superdome, one small testament to the will and determination to be safe during a potentially catastrophic hurricane even with limited resources to follow the miles of vehicles heading north. Thugs? Come on. The underlying story is much more interesting, compelling, sad, and important, the "cold fact that the fruits of recent economic growth had gone overwhelmingly to our richest citizens meant that millions of people continued to live in substandard housing, attend dysfunctional schools, travel slowly on broken-down public transportation systems, and die in overcrowded hospitals" (Keyssar 2005, B6), and that such patterns of wealth distribution have a long and deep history in our country.

Hurricane Katrina and the aftermath had the potential to open our eyes to what has existed all along but has been mired in silence: the silence of classist practices in the United States, the political silence of working-class and poor people, the social silencing of working-class and poor people. Multiple layers of such silences sound louder than drums when social structures quietly erode people's sense of self, prospects for schooling and employment, and opportunities to be valued in a democratic society. But alas, we still find ourselves unable to productively speak about social class, and only months after the horrific scenes from New Orleans donned magazine covers, newspaper pages, and our social imaginations, productive discussions and plans around poverty and strife in the working classes are once again silent.

Ms. Lockhart, Octavia, and Cadence all experienced versions of silence and silencing around social class issues in the last chapter. Perhaps Ms. Lockhart did not have access to ways of opening up a child's comment without sounding derogatory through the use of the available discourse around social class difference; therefore, Ms. Lockhart is silenced herself, unable to articulate something powerful and generative. Her silence on such topics sends implicit but constant messages about what is perceived as normal. Octavia received that perception of normalcy and decided to silence his own stories, and worse, ridicule those who voiced such experiences, like Cadence. And then there was Cadence, happy to express her understandings around things such as bullies and fathers in jail until someone (Octavia in this example) exposed the tabooed nature of her work. The result? More silence. She stopped telling the stories, making the connections to literature. The three are inextricably linked to one another's perceptions of social appropriateness based in social class expectations and the lack of language available to openly and generatively talk about experiences from outside a middle-class life. Such silence and the silencing of oneself and others have deep consequences for individuals and for working-class and poor folks as a collective. The remainder of this chapter will be devoted to various practices of silence and silencing as I use my experiences as a working-poor girl and my learning from St. Francis families, children, and teachers to explore some complications of a silencing phenomenon that is pervasive in our society.

■ The Silent Nature of Social Class Discrimination: St. Francis and Cocktail Parties

During an era when it is politically and socially unacceptable to sit in a teachers' lounge in the United States and talk about African American students as if they were inferior to Whites, or students who speak a language other than English at home, or boy students as superior to girls, it is still quite acceptable to make classist remarks without batting an eye:

- "We're working with the sludge of the gene pool here."

- "She [parent] doesn't have two nickels to rub together, how's she gonna sue the school?"

- And when a teacher was having dental problems she said, "I thought 'Oh no! I'm gonna look like all the people down there!'"

Down *there* is St. Francis.

The antipathy is transparent.

I could say the same for casual remarks at luncheons, cocktail parties, or friendly gatherings of middle-class and upper-middle-class, well-educated adults as conversations about someone being "rough around the edges" or from the "wrong side of town" or a casual, intended-to-be-comical description of a delivery man being able to "eat corn through a picket fence" in reference to his bucked teeth. These comments are class-based and reveal the underlying classist nature of our society where discourses around working-class and poor people are counterproductive at best, and at worst, blatant articulations of repugnance. A deprecating discourse, therefore, is alive and well when it comes to class hierarchies. What is missing is a discourse that is valuable, communal, and works toward a democratic ideal of equality. This missing discourse leaves a silent gap, a silence so loud that it suppresses those living working-class and poor lives.

All my life I struggled to shed my working-class/poor identity. Much like Octavia in the previous chapter, I *read* people early in life and understood the ways in which they might be looking at me, talking about me. My best friend in grade school wasn't allowed to play at my house—a trailer in a trailer park— for in the eyes of her parents, my childhood paradise was considered a danger zone. As I entered adolescence and met people from other parts of the city, a comment I often received was "you don't *look* like someone from *there*." *There* was my hometown, and the disbelief was obvious. The stereotypes are so strong and deep that it's nearly impossible for a middle-class or upper-class *someone* to believe that people from any of the many *theres* in the city (homes to working-class and poor people) can produce intelligent, attractive, insightful, and/or successful (in a mainstream sense) people.

Growing up in a working-poor family taught me politeness, however, and when I was with a group of middle-class others, I kept my comments to myself instead of upsetting the conversation of an entire table of people. As I smiled, nodded my head, and then stared silently when classist remarks were made, the voices in my mind were strong and vehement and I present one version of those voices to you here. As you read the following stream of consciousness, be sure to read fast and snappy with your eyebrows high, your eyes wide and your head swaying back and forth with what could be considered a really big attitude:

> Who in the hell do you think you are?! I have people in *my* family who have lost teeth and have never been able to have them fixed because they don't have money or insurance. I have a dad and uncles with long hair who like to smoke *pot* and drink Budweiser. I have a mother who likes *whiskey*. How do you like that? [smirk] My family rode Harleys long before they were trendy, and wears black T-shirts and denim jackets with chains on wallets. They go fishing and four-wheelin' for fun. What you see in *me* is fake, because I've tried to become like *you*. But the truth is that I love Harleys too, and I like to hang out in corner bars that are too damn smoky to see anything, with a jukebox in the corner playing Elvis, a pool table in the center, a 60-something barmaid who knows everyone's name, history, and sins, and a bowling game that I can dance on after I've downed a couple shots. How *dare* you judge people. Who do you think you are? When you judge *them* you judge *me*.

I was too kind though, to open up this Pandora's Box, kill the mood of a party, and make people believe that I was resentful—even when I was.

Times have changed however and I'm growing weary of the polite silence that working-class and poor people have been burdened with for far too long. Children begin bearing this burden at least as young as first grade in this study, and I don't want them to continue catering to people who act and speak in classist ways. It's time to speak up and put another truth on the table.

Shouting Back; Remaining Silent

"If people are going to kick you, don't just lie there. Shout back at them" (Allison 1988, 39). Dorothy Allison grew up a poor White girl in the South, learning many lessons from her mother including this one about talking back—getting your word in. Allison is a rare example of a critically acclaimed, White female writer who grew up in poverty in the United States. The rawness of her voice and the bareness of her stories ring true as I read her work, as I'm sure they resonate with other women who grew up in working-class or poor families. Her writing works as a response to her mother's order to "shout back at them," and it forces me to reconsider the politeness of silence I learned as a child and reflect on the roots of this phenomenon when I read the following excerpt from Allison:

> Push it down. Don't show it. Don't tell anyone what is really going on. We are not safe, I learned from my mama. There are people in the world who are, but they are not us. Don't show your stuff to anyone. Tell no one that your stepfather beats you. The things that would happen are too terrible to name. (1988, 36)

The classed nature of this forced silence is not uncommon. "We are not safe" can take on a variety of meanings. Institutionally speaking, poor people don't feel safe. The following examples are from St. Francis:

"Don't tell him that—tell him what he wants to hear," Heather's grandma told her daughter when she took the youngest baby to the pediatrician for a check-up.

"I'm always on the kids to keep the house clean or 888-KIDS [social service agency] will come and take 'em away," Rose's mom told me about the constant threat of social services intervening in private family matters—here, an untidy home.

Children hear and feel these threats early, yet they are rarely discussed openly. Over the years I spent with the girls they began to open up about the painful silence in which they lived their lives. Often this condition of living in silence was articulated in response to literature.

■ Silence and Fear

In the book, *The Color of My Words* (Joseph, 2002), Anna Rosa is a young girl writer in the Dominican Republic with whom the girls in this study found much affiliation. The following excerpt takes place as Anna Rosa is enjoying quiet time with her mother washing clothes in the river:

> Like when I asked him [Papi] if I could have a notebook just for writing my poems in it. He said, "Muchacha, your head is getting bigger than your hat."
> When I told Mami this on our next wash day, she laughed. But I could tell the laugh was only in her throat and not in her heart.
> "Your Papi says funny things sometimes, cariño," she said. "He's a dreamer."
> "A dreamer?" I asked. "How can you say that, Mami? All Papi does is sit on the porch and drink rum."
> Mami's hand shot out faster than a lizard under a rock. I felt the pain on my cheek before I realized what had happened.

"You have no hair on your tongue, chica. Be careful!"

I swallowed my tears and beat the clothes harder. Wash day had never been a day of sharp words and slaps. I felt as if Papi was a rock falling down from the hills and into our river. After the big splash, there was nothing but silence.

In daylight, silence is louder and angrier than at any other time. There are no sweet measures of silence such as night's stars, or evening's sunset, or morning's growing light. There is only bright, hard silence and it sounds louder than drums. (Joseph 2002, 5–6)

But I wanted to shake Mami's eyes open. Would we always be silent—the bright, hard daylight kind that is louder than drums? Couldn't I say what I wished—on paper? Even if it is only that Papi sits on the porch all day drinking rum? There! I shall never say it out loud again. Mami's slap will last a lifetime. (Joseph 2002, 9)

As I read this aloud to the girls sitting cross-legged on the floor entranced by Anna Rosa, Joanie yelled, "She got smacked!"

"Yes, she got smacked," I confirmed, "Why does her Mami tell her she must keep some things inside?" I asked.

Faith responded, "Because she gonna get smacked. She keeps saying out loud—what should I write? Should I write about him on the porch drinking rum?"

Just to make sure, I asked the girls, "Do you know what rum is?"

"Alcohol," replied Callie.

". . . and her mom kept on smackin' her because she didn't want other people to know their business," continued Faith.

"What do the rest of you think?" I asked.

"The same," said Callie.

Joanie added, "Or, someone could call the police and say, 'Papi is drinking alcohol' and they could take her right there. They take the kids away from them."

Knowing that Joanie had heard similar warnings in her home about someone coming to take the kids away, I asked a tough question, "So, has your family ever told you to not talk about something or write about something?"

"I can't talk about it or I'm gonna get in trouble," Faith reported.

"In our group no one gets in trouble. This is private information," I assured her since we were working in our small summer group for girls.

"My mom and dad. Not to tell other people's things. It's telling their business," continued Faith.

"That's the same thing that I tried to say, like if I say something about my mom or dad, I don't think I should tell other people their business," added Callie, "I feel bad about myself if I tell the things that my parents tell me not to tell people."

"It's a *secret*," Joanie told us.

"If someone says something in here, we don't say anything to anyone else. That's the deal we have," I had to reassure the girls even after two years.

Joanie added, "And don't say it at home either."

The girls had mostly accepted that I was not to be feared. I wouldn't judge them or their families based on the stories they told me, and I wouldn't contact authorities to have a family investigated based on something a girl shared.[1] This was a trust that the girls and their families rarely found in a person who looked, spoke, and acted middle class as I did. To be able to speak openly about the happenings in their lives seemed to be a great relief to the girls and, eventually, to some of their parents.

During the summer before the girls entered fifth grade, I sat with them at a park reminiscing about our work together when they were younger. Heather immediately talked about the feeling of security and safety in "talking about feelings." Each of the girls echoed Heather's sentiments that this was the most important part of the group's work and their favorite aspect of the dynamics; I read this as a breaking of a silence that the girls lived with day in and day out. I am not naïve and believe that I was privy to the most intimate, secret details of their lives, but I had gotten to know a great deal about their lived experiences through sanctioning topics that were typically taboo in elementary classrooms. Their trust in me was always fragile, however, and it didn't come easily or unchallenged, as I will discuss in Chapter 9.

The silent lives that must be lived by working-class and poor girls are in many ways lonely, isolated, and without credibility and validation from the larger society. Because of their fear of institutions and being judged harshly by others, young girls learn at a young age to keep family experiences a secret. Generations of keeping these lived experiences secret has led to a society that doesn't discuss realities of class-specific lives on the margins. The discourse around social class itself is silence—and it works as a powerful tool to hush the girls' lives in St. Francis, sweep them under the rug, pretend the differences are exaggerated, and blame the victim of a society grounded in inequity. A similar process successfully distorted and silenced stories from devastated New Orleans and permitted mainstream viewers to dismiss and forget them, reaffirming stereotypes of worthless and unworthy caricatures. Silence prevails.

■ Social Class and Self-Censoring in St. Francis

The nature of class inequality in the United States is taken for granted and assumed to be the way of the world: that some people "have it" (class) and some people don't. It is assumed by outsiders, and many residents themselves, that people just don't have it in St. Francis. Not having access to a discourse to talk about social class in overt and *productive* ways has left many people accepting their lot in life as fate—though certainly not unchallenged. It was as if many residents had come to the critical conclusion that the U.S. capitalistic economy was, indeed, dependent upon workers whose labor would come at little cost so profit margins would continue to increase for the upper crust. Therefore, those unfortunate enough to be born outside a realm of privilege without access to economic resources, educational opportunities, and social networks to help get a foot in the door of opportunity, would continue to struggle against great odds. And their children, born into loving families with much to offer experientially, would likely also struggle to gain access to the kinds of privilege taken for granted by so many other children.

This taken-for-granted view of one's world "goes without saying because it comes without saying" (Bourdieu 1994, 163) and takes a silent backseat to the official discourses of other, ostensibly more important things. At present in the United States, some of those official discourses are rallied around race and religion, immigration, terrorism, war, reforming social security, a rebounding economy, and corporate scandals. Social class issues, however, cut through all of these discourses as working-class and poor young citizens are heavily recruited[2] and shipped off to fight a war without sufficient supplies and technologies, as privatizing social security will hurt working-class and poor folks the most since they are less likely to have access to retirement plans in their places of work, and corporate scandals within the high-ranking officials trickle down to have devastating effects on those on the bottom rungs of such hierarchies. And when working-class and poor adults suffer, so do their children.

Official talk about living without electricity, ample supplies of food, communications, transportation, and real health care reform[3] is nonexistent—and what goes without saying is also not able to be said due to a lack of available discourse. Bourdieu, like others in the social sciences (e.g., Bernstein 1971; Freire 1970; Gee 1996; hooks 1994, 2000a, 2000b) suggests that the dominated classes can only begin to lift the censors they have used to silence their own experiences once they have the means of challenging what has been constructed as "real," valued, and assumed to be "normal." These censors are constantly reinforced through official discourses of institutions, as well as the continuous practice of silencing oneself and/or voicing "appropriate" responses aligned with mainstream values. In their responses to Anna Rosa's predicament in *The Color of My Words*, it was clear that very young school girls already had an understanding of mainstream values and institutional expectations and judgments as they censor themselves and silence their lives in order to protect themselves and their families from harm sure to come from others' discriminatory practices.

Thinking and talking about children's development of class consciousness and thus, identities within class-specific locations is one way to insert discussions of social class into official discourses around children, education, and community. A double-consciousness and self-surveillance of those who live in the working classes and poverty has been documented by many writers and researchers (Allison 2001; Anzaldua 1999; Bernstein 1971; Coles and Testa 2001; Freire 1970; hooks 1994, 2000a; Luttrell 1997; Schwartz 2002; Walkerdine et al. 2001). The absence of an easily accessible, productive way of talking about social class difference then, leaves most residents of St. Francis with quite sophisticated understandings and subtle readings of class relations that are not able to be articulated in a way that provides them and their community with an advantage. Instead, these critical thoughts around social class are often left untapped as people internalize the shame that is largely connected to those living in poverty. This shame leads many residents of St. Francis to express an ambiguous understanding of their own class positioning when speaking to outsiders (such as me) and to present themselves as somewhere in the "middle."

Girls and families in this study acknowledged class differences and demonstrated some critical consciousness of their own class positioning, but none spoke about it with conviction or a sense of a collective force. Formations were made, instead, around other concerns and an "us" against "them" practice had been developed when interacting with social service agents, police officers, teachers and principals, and even strangers driving by in nice cars who "think they're all *that*."

Exercise 5.1 A Conversation Around Silence

- Do you recognize a silence around social class issues? If so, how do you make sense of it? What does it mean in our society?

- How do your social class experiences impact your perceptions of and interactions with students? Could certain interactions be inadvertently imposing silence on students from working-class and/or poor families?

- Have you ever experienced an awkward or tense (maybe even silent) moment and recognized that it was a result of social class difference? What was it like?

- If you are from a working-class or poor background, how can you use your lived understandings of these marginalized positions to talk productively about social class marginalization?

● If you are from a more affluent background, how can you learn more about the complexities of living in our society on the margins of what is valued in the mainstream? How can you use your knowledge to create a space that is sensitive and responsive to class-specific lives?

This chapter has invited you to think deeply about the topics of social class and poverty in general, and consider how class is often constructed through silence in particular. Chapter 6 will provide an overview of critical literacy, a construct that offers tools for disrupting the silence in which marginalized groups live everyday lives. Not only a framework for considering education, critical literacy challenges us to reconsider the world and ask ourselves if the status quo, what we saw in the faces of tens of thousands from New Orleans and what you are learning about St. Francis, is socially just. If our answer is no, critical literacy challenges us to work toward change, opening up powerful spaces where voices from the margins are heard, valued, and worked with in solidarity toward social justice.

▓ Notes

1   I know this is a point of contention with many educators, so I want to clarify. I have never and would never contact child protective services before knowing (or "researching") the family, and having numerous conversations with others who also know the family well including administrators, school nurses, other teachers, community leaders, school secretaries, custodians, etc. One call can devastate a family and I would never make that decision on my own or based on one statement made by a child. I have, in fact, contacted authorities about a child after such conversations took place. This child was White, upper-middle class, and living in an affluent community where I once taught—not St. Francis.

2   Nearly two-thirds of all Army recruits in the year 2004 were from counties in which median household income is below the U.S. median (Tyson 2005).

3   It was estimated that 29.8 million people didn't have health insurance in 2004. Individuals living in a household with an income of less than $50,000 were more than twice as likely to have no health insurance than individuals living in a household with an income of more than $50,000 (DeNavas-Walt, Proctor, and Lee 2005).

6 | Breaking the Silence
Critical Literacy

S ilence is often used as a powerful vehicle for derailing language around the listener, a way to signify disagreement, doubt, misunderstanding, or even disgust. Power can also be exercised through silence by signaling affiliation, understanding, or even admiration. What we don't often acknowledge, however, is that silences are filled with unspoken language, images, affect. The girls' silence around their home lives was in response to what they had heard from their families time and again about child protection services coming "to take kids away"; words and ideas, then, populated those silent spaces created by the girls. Critical literacy offers the tools to investigate language constructions, including silence, through the assumption that anything that has been constructed through language is saturated with perspectives or ideological beliefs and therefore can be deconstructed and better understood. Such constructions could take infinite forms including a social interaction, an internet website, a children's book, a television commercial, a sitcom, an email, or a newspaper article.

James Gee (2001) considers using critical literacy practices in social interactions "socially-perceptive literacy," and "critical media literacy" is used to describe critical literacy practices in reading media (Alvermann, Moon, and Hagood 1999); therefore, an infinite number of ways to engage critical literacy practices exist, and some will be explored in this chapter beginning with a scenario that took place while I was a teacher-researcher in St. Francis. I connect this St. Francis scene with memories of my own childhood and more contemporary happenings in my family. Rooting our understandings of critical literacy practices in everyday events is one way to explore the construct that is the focus of this chapter. Following illustrations around police-community relations, the United States criminal justice system, and social class, I present a brief history of critical literacy and introduce three layers of questioning that can provide an entry to critical literacy practices: perspective, power, and positioning. A major emphasis of this chapter will be the importance of beginning with students' lives to construct critical literacy practices.

■ A Scene from St. Francis

It was lunchtime and the fast eaters were outside Bruger Elementary School on the blacktop playground beneath a dark autumn sky. Students were shooting basketballs through netless hoops, swinging by the bends in their legs on the monkey bars, paralyzing peers during freeze tag, and yelling obscenities to friends and used-to-be-friends through hands cupped tightly around mouths. Seemingly from nowhere, a twenty-something-year-old White male sprinted across the tarred surface, coattail flapping in the wind. Not far behind him ran two police officers demanding that he stop. The principal of Bruger Elementary watched the scene and described it to me later as he said, "I was rooting for the good guys and all the kids were rooting for the bad guy."

The dichotomy was clear: Good guy—Bad guy. Us—Them. Self—Other. The "good guys" from the principal's perspective were the "guys" representing a respectable institution in the larger society: the police officers. The "bad guy" was the one running from the police. No one knew why the young male was running, but the assumption was that he had broken the law in some way, making him "bad," and he was trying to avoid paying the price for his crime by running from the officers. The "bad guys," from the students' point of view, may very well have been the "cops" or "pigs" as they were often called in St. Francis. The police officers[1] were often viewed as perpetrators, chasing a good guy from the neighborhood for no good reason.

Such a scene was not uncommon in St. Francis, and the good guy—bad guy dichotomy was played out in conversations around the community. According to many of the residents the good guy was one of their own and the bad guy was a representative from an institution who was intervening in their lives in some unwanted way. The cops, in particular, have been recognized as stereotypical others who violate and dehumanize St. Francis residents in many ways including verbal insult and physical abuse. Bonnie, Callie's mother, told me about a police officer who screamed at her to get her "White trashy ass off the street." Many residents had conceptualized the police as a group of people who judged St. Francis residents as no-good White trash, and St. Francis residents retaliated with their own constructions of the cops as the other who were lazy, uninvolved, not interested in helping the community, and low on the totem pole when it comes to species: "Pigs." These adult understandings of police officers and "The Law" as an institution were passed on both implicitly and explicitly to children who were enculturated to continue constructing and judging in similar ways.

■ A Scene from My Life

I grew up afraid of the cops, or the pigs as my family called them. They locked people up, beat people down, punished with tickets that were unable to be paid, picked on poor people, and ridiculed family members. When shadows lengthen and darkness falls in my hometown, my grandma makes her way to the bedroom and her bedside table where the honeywood surface is neatly occupied by a Bible, a book (*Why Bad Things Happen to Good People*), a lamp, and a police scanner—the trusty gadget from where static-filled voices come to keep her informed of the happenings on the street. She goes to bed each night selectively listening for familiar names of people and streets that might signify someone she loves is in trouble and in need of her help. This ritual has proven helpful a number of times as she has heard (on separate occasions) the names of my brother, uncle, cousins, and stepdad, and immediately called the courthouse to see when they could be bailed out and how much money it was going to take to do so. Having known about the arrests early gave my grandmother time to contact relatives and friends to gather the cash necessary (at least in most cases) to get our loved ones out of the pokey as soon as possible. The self-other dichotomy was always clear to my family and me. Those we loved were the good guys, and the perpetrators (cops in these cases) were the bad guys (with rare exceptions). How could someone who would do anything for anyone in his family be considered the bad guy? I know why the students were rooting for the so-called "bad guy," he is representative of them; of Us.

For years I carried a complex range of beliefs and feelings about the seemingly bitter rivalry between my family (and much of the community) and the police. At times I simply placed blame on my own family members, other times I despised the police. It wasn't until late adolescence that I began to question and challenge the actions of police in working-class and poor communities. Too often news reports of police brutality (and ensuing riots) are situated solely in race and racial tensions between White officers and African American citizens (e.g., Harlem riots of 1935; Detroit and Newark, 1967; Los Angeles, 1991; and Cincinnati, 2001) without investigating the class dynamics at play in this practice of social control. Clearly, African American males in particular are over-whelmingly a target of discrimination when it comes to the U.S. justice system with 4,919 out of every 100,000 Black males incarcerated versus 717 out of every 100,000 of their White counterparts.[2] But working-class and poor males (Black, White, and Hispanic) are also a target of such discrimination. Of all male prisoners in mid-year 2002, 90 percent were earning an income of $25,000 or less while 69 percent were living below the poverty level at the time of their arrest (Child Welfare League of America). White, African American, and Hispanic working-class and poor women face similar challenges, but they don't yet find themselves incarcerated as often as their male counterparts. In mid-year 2004, 103,310 females were incarcerated (U.S. Department of Justice) and the majority of those were earning low incomes.[3]

▦ What Does This Have To Do with Critical Literacy? Challenging What Seems to be "Natural"

Social class does matter in police-community relations and understanding such issues depends on the exploration of *power, perspective, and positioning.* For example, in the summer of 2005, a newspaper in Panama City, Florida reported that a Highway Patrol spokesperson discussing a new minimum speed limit of fifty miles per hour on the highway told the *Gainesville Sun* that "officers more likely will overlook slowpoke grandmothers than they will lower classes—people driving "trashy" vehicles that can't go much faster, people who are always suspect."[4] The *perspective* of this spokesperson is that folks who can only afford "trashy" vehicles that might have difficulty maintaining at least fifty miles per hour are already "suspect"; the implication being that poor and working-class people are assumed to be guilty and in need of police intervention. The unstated assumption, then, is that folks who can afford newer (not trashy) vehicles receive the benefit of the doubt when it comes to questioning whether or not they are breaking any laws. The *power* exercised by the police officers, then, is not to harass presumed "innocent" elderly women who drive slowly, but instead to have the new law as an excuse to pull over working-class and poor people for a closer look. More so, since such people are the targets of suspicion in the first place, officers assume they may find additional reasons to reprimand and fine drivers. The drivers of such vehicles are *positioned* as suspects for breaking laws and the officers are *positioned* as having the power to decide who will and will not be permitted to break the new minimum speed limit law. The elderly women who are not driving trashy cars are positioned as careful, slow drivers, who are otherwise assumed to be law-abiding citizens. Perhaps the perspective of the Highway Patrol is that working-class and poor people can exercise less *power* when engaging with institutions, therefore they will be less likely to challenge the officers in ways that would be perceived as legitimate in the justice system. This is clearly a case of profiling and discrimination based on the perception of social class status.

Considering perspective, power, and positioning are important aspects of critical literacy. These tools offer the opportunity to dig deeper into an issue such as police-community relations, that for so long seemed cut-and-dry and grounded exclusively in racism. The feeling of powerlessness when dealing with the police and justice system as a whole can be overwhelming,[5] but for working-class and poor people it can also be assumed to be "just the way it is."

"Just the way it is" represents a social and political practice as natural and therefore unchallengeable. Barbara Comber suggests that challenging what is perceived to be natural or neutral is a crucial practice in critical literacy, and I would argue that opening up such conversations is one way of breaking a culture of silence that can overwhelm people who are consistently positioned as outsiders of a mainstream society. All cultural practices, including perceptions and stereotypes of categories such as gender, race, class, religion, sexuality, and so forth have been created by people, therefore people can challenge narrow representations and work toward change. Engaging in critical conversations around issues that impact one's daily life may be difficult—it may be easier to pretend a discriminatory practice doesn't exist rather than to think deeply and articulate the hurtful, dehumanizing facts of a stratified society, especially if one does not feel she or he has the power to change unjust practices. The alternative to conversation, however, is continued silence and acceptance of what has been naturalized in our society.

Just as it has helped me to understand some of the complexities of social relations, critical literacy gives me the tools to think more insightfully and reflect more critically on how concrete experiences such as these impact students' and families' willingness, or resistance, to connect with school workers and believe in the broader goals of education. Through the teaching of a critical literacy stance in the classroom, educators can help working-class and poor students break the silence of their lives. Critical literacy practices can open up spaces where students can claim value in their experiences and critique mainstream ideals that marginalize them and their families. These practices can provide students with the tools to reconsider social and political "realities" and place their voices in the center of conversations where they have too often been left out.

For the students in this study, critical literacy cracked open a curriculum that was overwhelmingly focused on middle-class lives, experiences, and values, practices that have been naturalized through children's literature, films, sit-coms, magazines, and advertising. Students began to question and re-create seemingly "safe" children's texts such as *Henry and Mudge* (Chapter 10), photograph their community as representative of a "normal" life (Chapter 11), publish pieces of writing on topics that might be considered taboo in many primary classrooms, and insert their lived realities into school-based discussions with a sense of entitlement where there was once silence (Chapter 4). But what exactly *is* critical literacy and where did it come from? The following sections will present a brief overview of the history and development of critical literacy, as well as an attempt at a definition and an exploration of what I call three layers of critical literacy practices.

▣ A Brief Historical Perspective

Critical literacy[6] has grown largely out of critical theory[7] and its intersections with feminist theory,[8] poststructuralist theories,[9] theories around language and power,[10] and education as a liberatory practice.[11] Further, it is one attempt at transforming a powerful theoretical perspective into classroom practice. Theory doesn't easily transfer into practice and critical literacy is no exception, partly because the overlapping theories are complex, multilayered, and embedded within knowledge bases constructed by theorists across time. Ongoing research and rethinking around critical literacy practices in elementary, high school, and university classrooms, however, is widespread and stimulating, and stems a great deal from the work of Paulo Freire.

Paulo Freire is considered a pioneer of critical theory and critical literacy. A major goal of his work with adult literacy learners was *praxis*, or reflective practice that engages critical rethinkings and reimaginings; critical reflection and action. From a modest background in Brazil, Freire worked with adult literacy learners from marginalized classes, or *peasants*, teaching them to articulate their readings of the *world*, which later helped them to read the *word* in their adult literacy classes. He believed that people living under oppressive conditions felt and understood social, political, and economic injustice, but had been positioned in such a way that the larger society would not respect their perspectives, and that many peasants themselves appropriated the belief that they were uneducated and not worthy of having powerful knowledge (Freire 1998; Freire and Macedo 1987).

Literacy students in Freirean-inspired classes were encouraged to talk about their experiences in the underclasses and construct sophisticated understandings around the power relations that upheld a stratified society where a person's worth depended on wealth and status. These discussions led to literacy teachers choosing relevant words or phrases to ground literacy lessons (such as *brick*—a material used by many of the workers in one particular class). The foundation of the work, then, was to learn details of students' lives, develop their abilities to articulate what they knew to be true about the world around them, and draw from these experiences to construct reading and writing lessons.

Freire's work landed him in exile as the government of Brazil thought it too progressive, politicized, and dangerous to the political, social, and economic status quo. Educating the masses and building critically literate groups of people who had been historically oppressed could lead to organized resistance and upset the power structure. Though he later returned to Brazil and served as Secretary of Education within a new government, Freire worked across the globe in developing countries to stimulate, organize, and lead literacy campaigns among the poorest and most disadvantaged people.

Freire's theories and practices were not perfect, however, and though they laid the groundwork for future research, practice, and theory building in critical literacy, his books have not been safe from critique. One example is his nearly exclusive references to men, not women, and their lived experiences. For a scholar engaged in questioning the status quo, Freire did not critically reflect on his location as a White male and how such locations are privileged. Feminist critiques, then, of Freire's work are strong and worthy of reading (e.g., Weiler 1994) and later in his life he acknowledged this oversight and encouraged continued critique and rethinking of his work. Such reconsideration has fueled yet another critique: Freire's early commitment to learning the language-worlds of literacy students and using those worlds (and words) to construct literacy lessons falls disturbingly short in some of his later work as he and colleagues attempted to reproduce strategies that had been productive with particular groups of people. For example, the teachers' decision making was replaced by the use of mass-produced workbooks that guided literacy lessons (e.g., Freire and Macedo 1987). The underlying assumption is that similar groups of people experience oppression in similar ways, therefore the lessons can be preplanned. Though this may have seemed to be a quick fix to provide support to under- and unprepared teachers, it stripped the student-teacher dialogue of what was most important: *the understanding of students' lives outside the literacy classes*. Centering conversations and lessons around predetermined texts focuses critical literacy practices on *textual* practices, while perpetuating the marginalization of students' lived realities.

Like the work of some critical literacy researchers (Alvermann and Hong Xu 2003; Clarke 2005; Dyson 1993, 1997; Epstein 1993; Hicks 2001, 2004; Vasquez

2004) a key argument in this book is that critical literacy practices are best grown from what students do and say, and from what we know about our students, their families, and their communities. Part of the *problem* with this situated view of critical literacy is that teachers and teacher educators cannot always plan curricula in advance, that we, as Paulo Freire put it in a conversation with the revolutionary educator Myles Horton, "make the road by walking" (Bell, Gaventa, and Peters 1990, 6). Comber and Simpson (2001) emphasize the local nature of critical literacy practices when they write:

> Critical literacy resists any simplistic or generic definitions because its agenda is to examine the relationships between language practices, power relations, and identities—and this analysis involves grappling with specific local conditions. (271)

Grappling with specific local conditions means taking the time and investing the effort to *understand* local conditions. Versions of the suggested research project in Chapter 2 of this book could support ongoing research in the communities where we work and with the families and children for whom we work. bell hooks, an African American female scholar in Black feminist theory and critical pedagogue, reflected on her experiences as a child who was taught by African American women who knew her community and family well.

■ Critical Literacy: Starting with Lives

In her book *Teaching to Transgress: Education as the Practice of Freedom* (1994), bell hooks reflects on her own experiences as a young girl in a changing world. Attending a rural segregated school for Black children, hooks experienced a connectedness with the Black teachers and the lasting feeling that education was (or should be) a practice of freedom. Though she recognized the social class differences between herself and more affluent students and the superior treatment they received, hooks (2000) found solidarity and comfort in her small school where Black children were taught and cared for by Black teachers. This experience was altered drastically when forced integration sent hooks to a school attended by Whites. Recalling the familiar, intergenerational, empowering spaces of her earliest educational memories, hooks writes:

> Almost all our teachers at Booker T. Washington were black women. They were committed to nurturing intellect so that we could become scholars, thinkers, and cultural workers—black folks who used our "minds." We learned early that our devotion to learning, to a life of the mind, was a counter-hegemonic act, a fundamental way to resist every strategy of white racist colonization. Though they

did not define or articulate these practices in theoretical terms, my teachers were enacting a revolutionary pedagogy of resistance that was profoundly anticolonial . . . my teachers made sure they "knew" us. They knew our parents, our economic status, where we worshipped, what our homes were like, and how we were treated in the family. I went to school at a historical moment where I was being taught by the same teachers who had taught my mother, her sisters, and . brothers. My effort and ability to learn was always contextualized within the framework of generational family experience. Certain behaviors, gestures, habits of being were traced back. (1994, 2–3)

The themes running throughout the second part of this quote, the practices that allowed teachers to teach in revolutionary ways in the classroom, echo those written about in this book. hooks felt her teachers knew her well, and the examples she uses are all from outside the classroom. Parents, social class status, places of worship, homes, family, and generational behaviors and habits of being were considered the precious pieces of a student that the teachers knew. This kind of knowing about a student's life cannot take place in a classroom alone, it takes time, patience, and energy beyond the four walls of the institution called school—and beyond one's identity as a traditional *teacher* within those walls, as teachers work in humble ways with families to share power and knowledge.

The classroom pedagogy hooks reflected upon as being antiracist and anticolonial could be considered in today's educational literature as a kind of *critical literacy* (e.g., Comber 1998, 2001; Lankshear and McLaren 1993; Luke and Freebody 1996). Hilary Janks (2000) developed a matrix of interdependent concepts fundamental in critical literacy work in the classroom: domination, access, diversity, and design.[12]

- Domination is focused on the deconstruction of language and text that is used for maintaining power over others.

- Access refers to the ongoing issue in the teaching of Language Arts: ensuring students have access to dominant languages, discourses, and practices without devaluing students' home and community ways with words.

- Diversity is grounded in the assumption that difference is valuable to a group and when embraced, such diversity can lead to innovation.

- Design zeroes in on the productive role power can play when literacies are used to reconstruct social and political relations through challenging inequity and oppression.

In hooks' reflection (hooks 1994), one can locate Janks' four concepts in the work of the teachers: We can imagine that hooks' teachers were politically motivated to deconstruct dominant discourses (domination) while they ensured students had access to those dominant forms of literacy that would help them succeed in the larger society (access). The students' diverse lived realities were known, validated, and even researched (diversity), and *this* is where productive curricular work began, harnessing the diversity of children's lives to design, or *reconstruct* what is possible (design).

■ Definition, Please?

What critical literacy *is* has been more challenging to articulate than what it *isn't* (Comber 2001) since embracing a critical literacy stance is not a specific strategy, host of activities, or even a replacement for progressive pedagogies such as process writing and genre instruction, but rather a *perspective*, a political stance around issues of language and literacy. Comber and Kamler (1997) argue that

> What a critical perspective does offer teachers is a way to think about what it is students are learning to read and write, what they do with that reading and writing, and what that reading and writing does to them and their world.

Critical literacy, then, does not exclude many typical forms of literacy teaching and learning in progressive pedagogies in the United States such as the read-aloud, shared reading, independent reading, reading share, and process writing. The difference is the work we do within these sites of teaching and learning and how we think about that work.

Over time, semantics and considerations have shifted a bit within the field of critical literacy, but a standing argument remains that a *social view* of reading is necessary and that teachers who understand this perspective will pay more attention to the social and political contexts within reading, writing, and language broadly (Bomer and Bomer 2001; Christensen 2000; Comber 2002). This key argument is grounded in teachers focusing on the diverse cultural and discursive resources of the children, and Comber believes that teachers are central to the work and should be considered "cultural workers" (2002). I would add that students are also positioned as cultural workers in their own right, perhaps they will be working to understanding themselves, their social relations within family, school, community, and the larger global context; and I envision teachers as engaging in the same sort of self-reflective work. The following section will point to the importance of such cultural work and the rooting of critical literacy in the lives of the students in each of our classrooms.

■ Starting with Lives in St. Francis

More than a year after we first met, I sat with Cadence's mother Lori and asked her to reflect on her school experiences and what could be different for her daughter and other girls at Bruger Elementary School. She looked at me hard (never sure whether or not to trust in full) and then began articulating part of her philosophy of education:

> I'm young, I remember when I was in high school—people didn't associate with the teachers . . . you gotta make them want to come, you gotta catch their interest, you know, once you catch that interest of the child, you got 'em for good, but you gotta figure out what is going to catch them. I think you come at them on their level—okay—and you let them express themselves at their own level—what they wanna express themselves about, you will have that child—you will, they will be just like a book, you can open them right up. You have to find what it is about them—and nine times out of ten, with kids it *is* their life.

Lori's vision of how school should be for Cadence and girls like her is closely related to the writings of critically focused educators such as Paulo Freire, Myles Horton, and bell hooks. She argues that teachers have to make kids *want* to come to school through catching their interest, which is likely to be their lives. And when teachers know students' lives and encourage children to express themselves "at their own level" then they will "have" those students, they will have captured their interest, motivated them, convinced them that education is relevant to them and powerful. Grounding a pedagogy in the lived experiences of students is crucial to begin overt processes of merging home lives with the dominant discourses of schooling. This pedagogical grounding is not simple, however, and takes a great amount of sensitivity and effort on the part of educators. Creating a classroom environment where *talk* is privileged and encouraged will set the stage for rich, personal discussions that are most often based in the language of the students ("nonstandard," slang, and all) and open to insightful analyses by the students and teacher. These insights can help teachers choose instructional tools (e.g., books, films, websites, projects, field trips, discussion and writing topics like the topic of "jail" highlighted in Chapter 4) and make decisions about the direction of critical literacy that are in direct response to students' lives and desires while helping students challenge their own assumptions and understandings about the world.

■ Finally, Defining Critical Literacy

Critical literacy is like a pair of eyeglasses that allows one to see beyond the familiar and comfortable; it is an *understanding* that language practices and texts are always informed by ideological beliefs and perspectives whether conscious or otherwise. It is a habit of *practice* to think beyond and beneath text, investigating issues of power and whose interests are being served by texts, whose interests are not being served, and why. A critical literacy lens focuses on three interrelated *layers*: perspective, positioning, and power; and engages in three foundational *tenets*: deconstruction, reconstruction, and social action. The following section will present three layers of critical literacy practices, with the tenets being a focus of Chapter 7.

■ Three Layers of Critical Literacy Inquiry: Perspective, Positioning, and Power

A critical literacy stance assumes that:

- All texts (i.e., spoken, written, performed, and multimodal) are constructed by people who are informed by particular ideologies—they are entrenched in *perspective*.

- All texts make the experiences of some people seem more valuable than others, enabling some to exercise power more freely than others—they contribute to social and political *positioning*.

- All texts grow from language practices, which are embedded in relations of social and political differentials that are distributed across a hierarchy in society—they are always indicative and productive of *power*.

Therefore, when analyzing the St. Francis playground-and-police scenario from a critical literacy stance, we ask about perspectives of the speaker, text, and audience, positioning of people within and outside the text, and how power mediates the text itself and our thinking about it. We want to consider multiple perspectives, perspectives of everyone in the text and perspectives of those not present (for example, family members who learn that a foot chase has crisscrossed their children's playground such as in the scene from St. Francis). Considering this pushes us to think about mainstream perspectives that are often taken for granted, or "naturalized," in a White middle-class world and those perspectives that are most often silenced. Critical literacy helps to break this silence as it opens up spaces for mainstream and marginalized perspectives to be considered in the name of social justice.

Consider the following questions about the playground-and-police scenario, thinking specifically about the words of the principal, "I was rooting for the good guys and all the kids were rooting for the bad guy."

1. From what perspective is the principal speaking?
2. How does the language used position the police officers in relation to the running man?
3. How does the language used position the running man in relation to the police officers?
4. How does the language used position the principal in relation to the police officers, running man, and the community?
5. How does the language used position the "kids"?
6. How might the story read from one of the kid's perspective?
7. How might the story read from the perspective of one of the officers?
8. Which version of the story is most likely to be accepted as "truth" in mainstream, White middle-class society? Why? What role does power play in such "true" representations?
9. How then, is power distributed in this single event? Is power used in the name of domination or in the name of social justice?

▮ Critical Literacy and Lives

Critical literacy is building a way of life through active engagement *with* life—a way of noticing "What's wrong with this picture?" a way of asking oneself, "How is power being exercised here and how does that shape what we're doing?" In this chapter we have considered a brief history of critical literacy and the importance of growing critical literacy practices out of students' lives. Using perspective, positioning, and power, we have worked through one example of employing critical literacy practices to help us see beyond the familiar and comfortable mainstream view of a police chase across a playground in a working-poor neighborhood. These three layers will be elaborated upon in Chapter 7 as I situate them within a familiar story of a marginalized character and the three tenets[13] of critical literacy practices.

▮ Notes

1 One significant exception to this rule was an officer who worked the beat of St. Francis regularly. I watched this African American middle-aged man in admiration as he attended and interacted at monthly community meetings in an observably

humble and respectful manner. The community members seemed to believe he was working in solidarity with them, and when they had loud complaints about other officers, they ran to him for assistance. Most interesting, to me, was that he was one of the only African American officers in the predominantly White neighborhood. Sharing skin color, then, did not help either officers or residents construct any affinity for one another. The abuse and mistreatment of White residents by White police officers is not something we see in the news, but it certainly points to social class as a factor that is rarely considered. Most of the unrest set off by perceived police abuse of African Americans is also concentrated in poor, urban centers—indicating working-class and poor residents as the target of abuse, their race only compounding the oppressive forces.

2 U.S. Department of Justice statistics at mid-year 2004, www.ojp.usdoj.gov/bjs/prisons.htm

3 www.financeproject.org/Publications/lowincomemothersissuenote.htm

4 Editorial, Panama City News Herald, June 17, 2005.

5 Particularly given the fact that the United States leads the world in rates of incarceration. There were 2,135,901 prisoners in jail or prison at the end of 2004, not counting juveniles in detention centers or those in military detention centers. This rate of 724 prisoners per 100,000 people is higher than any other country in the world. Second place is the Russian Federation at 581 prisoners per 100,000 people (International Centre for Prison Studies, www.prisonstudies.org).

6 See Comber 1998, 2001, 2002; Comber, Cormack, and O'Brien 1998; Comber and Kamler 1997; Fehring and Green 2001; Janks 2000; Lankshear and McLaren 1993; Muspratt, Luke, and Freebody 1997.

7 See Giroux, Lankshear, and McLaren 1996.

8 See Hill Collins 2000; hooks 2000; Smith 1997; Weiler 1994.

9 See Foucault 1990; Weedon 1997.

10 See Fairclough 1995; Gee 1996, 1999; Heath 1983; Rogers 2003.

11 See Finn 1999; Freire 1998; Freire and Shor 1987; hooks 1994, 2003.

12 These four concepts are reflected and embedded in the tenets and layers of critical literacy I offer in this book.

13 Deconstruction, Reconstruction, and Social Action.

7 | Critical Literacy

A Frame for Thinking, Planning, and Enacting

I n *The True Story of the 3 Little Pigs! By A. Wolf* written by Jon Scieszka, a well-known, mainstream story is reconstructed from the perspective of the wolf. The book begins like this:

> Everybody knows the story of the Three Little Pigs. Or at least they think they do. But I'll let you in on a little secret. Nobody knows the real story, because nobody has ever heard *my* side of the story. (1)

The *real* story continues and Alexander T. Wolf claims that his "Big Bad Wolf" persona has been constructed by people who have never considered his perspective, and in particular, by people who don't understand the nature of wolves' diets; he insists that if cheeseburgers were cute little animals "like bunnies and sheep and pigs" then humans would be considered Big and Bad too. However, the day the Three Little Pigs' lives were forever memorialized, Mr. Wolf was not intentionally looking to eat any pigs. Instead, he was home baking a cake for his grandmother, realized he needed sugar, and headed out to the neighbor's to borrow a cup. All the while, Mr. Wolf was fighting a cold and sneezing terribly.

The first neighbor's house was made of sticks and when Mr. Wolf knocked on the door it fell in. The neighbor (who happened to be a pig) didn't respond to his calls so he started to walk away when a sneezing fit overcame him. Huffing and puffing, Mr. Wolf let go of a sneeze that blew the whole house down. And can you believe it? The pig was killed in the accident—"dead as a doornail" in the middle of the mess. Unable to turn his back on a tasty-looking dinner ("think of it as a big cheeseburger just lying there"), the wolf indulged.

The second neighbor was busy shaving his "chinny-chin-chin" and Mr. Wolf was prepared to move on to the third house when a sneeze started coming on. He tried to cover his mouth, of course, but the sneeze was too powerful, "And you're not going to believe it, but this guy's house fell down just like his brother's," the Wolf said, and the pig was killed in the mishap. Not wanting food to spoil, Mr. Wolf helped himself to seconds.

And finally he made his way with measuring cup in hand to the third house, a brick house, only to find an impolite neighbor unwilling to loan sugar. Adding insult to injury, the pig neighbor yelled, "And your old granny can sit on a pin!" Well that did it for Mr. Alexander T. Wolf, no one was going to disgrace his granny. In a rage, Mr. Wolf tried to break down the door, huffing and puffing with a sneeze on the way the whole time. And that's when the police officers pulled up, the news reporters arrived, and a new story was created.

Along with the story, a photo was printed of Mr. Wolf dancing about in a huffing-puffing manner trying to bust down a door and attempting to hold in a sneeze.

Mr. Alexander T. Wolf was "framed."

Exercise 7.1 We Are All Being Framed

The metaphor of being "framed" is useful in thinking about critical literacy, the three tenets (Deconstruction, Reconstruction, and Social Action) and the three layers (Perspective, Positioning, Power). Consider the following questions in relation to a snapshot photograph you have:

- What is inside the frame of the photograph?

- Inside the frame, what (or who) is centered? What (or who) is decentered, or on the margins?

- What is outside the frame of the photograph?

- What is the message, or the story, being conveyed by the photographer?

- How does the photographer's perspective change the story that can be told and/or read from the photograph?

- The photographer exercised power in decision making, how was this power used? Is the power used to privilege one version of a story over another? Is the power used to offer a perspective that seems "alternative?" Is the power used to tell the same kind of story over again (a mainstream story)?

● Do you view this photograph in a different light after considering these questions? If so, how?

■ Joanie's Photograph

The photograph below was taken by Joanie during the summer after her second-grade year as she took me on a tour around her home.

The objects inside this photograph include used tires, rims, and some small pieces of wood. Centered, and given most of the attention here, are the used tires piled on top of one another, on the margins are small pieces of wood. What lies outside the frame, however, is unknown by the viewer who is unfamiliar with the context and the photographer, but since I am familiar with both (like you are with your own snapshots), I can narrate some of that here: The tires are situated within a wooded area on a hillside behind a billboard that shades the sidewalk in front of Joanie's apartment. The "woods," as they're known to Joanie and her cousins, is off-limits terrain filled with adventure. The tires, from Joanie's perspective at the time she took the photograph, are a dangerous addition to this play area and her centering of them in this photograph is a statement of anger. Even though she and her cousins were not permitted to play here they often did, and though they find the woods in general a place for fun, Joanie recognized the danger in using it as a dumping ground. This didn't keep her from occasionally walking or sitting on the tires, of course, but she did choose the pile as the subject of this photograph and the center of discontent with her recreational space. Joanie is using her power as the creator of this photo (text) to represent a very specific piece of her playspace—not her favorite thing to do, or something she likes, but to put on display something that makes her angry: she intended a particular story with this picture.

In addition to the information to which I was privy through Joanie's articulations during this walking tour, I know much about the community and can add more context to this photograph: it was taken in the only greenspace within walking distance from Joanie's apartment without crossing a major intersection, the tires weren't all dumped at once and the pile has grown over time. Inside the frame, the lens is focused on a part of the community perceived by Joanie as being negative, outside the frame there are children playing and being creative with the space available to them; there are families joking with children, and there is a happenin' café, Utopia, across the street where people gather to eat cheese coneys and burgers.

Joanie's photograph represents a particular slice of life—a slice that is neither normal nor abnormal, typical nor atypical; it's simply a slice. This photograph can never be used to typify or essentialize experience, then, or Joanie and her community members could do just what the Wolf did and claim to have been "framed" without other truths being told (which often happens in St. Francis and to residents). There is too much movement, too much complexity beyond the edges of this photograph to allow it to be representative, much like a snapshot could not be representative of your whole life. History, culture, and social relations are much too messy to be neatly framed, much too alive to be frozen into representation. At least some of this messiness can be accounted for and analyzed within the layers and tenets of critical literacy.

▪ Messiness Inside and Outside the Frame: Thinking About Critical Literacy

Just as the photograph exercise pushed you to think about the messiness of what may otherwise seem a straightforward and simple text, similar work helps us to do the same with books, advertisements, television shows, media, conversations, and other textual representations. The three tenets and layers of critical literacy that I offer here are inextricably intertwined and offer tools necessary to move beyond the superficial and surface level of texts of all kinds

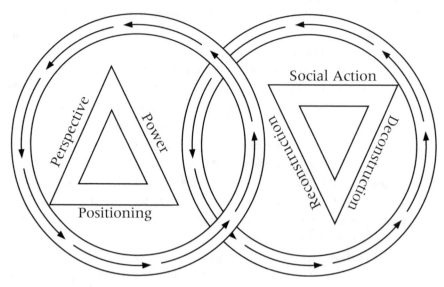

FIG 7–2 *Critical Literacy*

(see Figure 7–2). Their relationships to one another make thinking about critical literacy fascinating, intriguing, and empowering while at the same time their interconnectedness may challenge those of us trying to decide what to do with our students on Monday morning. It is never possible to focus on all six aspects outlined here at one time; rather, one tenet or layer may be foregrounded for a short time before moving on to another and then another. Making the decision about what to foreground, when to do so, and why such a decision is important is what I will attempt to assist you with, though I will offer no clear-cut answers or prescriptions. What I will say and continue to emphasize is that those decisions will rely heavily upon your knowledge of your students and their lives inside and outside the classroom.

■ Tenets of Critical Literacy: Deconstruction, Reconstruction, and Social Action

Mr. Wolf reconstructed a mainstream story to place his perspective at the center of attention. For him to make the decision that a reconstruction needed to take place however, he must have engaged in some level of deconstruction of the original story and realized that his perspective was not taken into consideration. And, finally, by releasing this new version of the "real story," Mr. Wolf is engaging in social action: He is working toward persuading people to reconsider the age-old tale of the three little pigs victimized by a Big Bad Wolf.

Deconstruction: Texts and Identities

Deconstruction is the tenet of critical literacy that promises to keep us aware that all texts are constructed and therefore can be deconstructed, taken apart bit-by-bit to unveil power, perspective, and positioning. All "selves," or identities, are also constructed—constructed by oneself, those closest to us, and by outside cultural, political, and social forces. Thus, identities can also be deconstructed (and, hence, reconstructed). Mr. Wolf recognized that the original *Three Little Pigs* story represented a singular perspective, assigning power of domination to him as the predator, and positioning him as the criminal in the case, while the pigs were positioned as innocent victims with no role in their own demise (but remember, two *did* build homes that were demolished by a single sneeze and one *clearly* disrespected the wolf's aged granny). Though he did not write explicitly about his deconstruction of the text, Mr. Wolf had certainly engaged in this tenet in his understanding of journalistic politics (a sick wolf baking a cake for granny isn't an exciting story), and the criminal justice system.

Working in critical ways to interrogate texts has been likened to "peeling an onion" (Foss 2002), and the metaphor works when considering the fact that all are embedded with multiple layers of meaning. In deconstruction, we work toward peeling layers away from the text in an attempt to understand better how various people or groups of people are being positioned, and how such is occurring through the text.

Deconstruction of Texts: Classroom Possibilities

- Read a text (e.g., book, textbook, poem, article, letter, etc.) with the following questions in mind: What voices are important here? What voices seem unimportant? What is presented as "normal" in this text? How can you tell? Who might feel comfortable reading this text and why? Who might feel uncomfortable reading this text and why?

- Encourage readers to locate disconnections or feelings of disconnect as they read. This disconnect can lead to questioning and challenging of the author's perspective and uses of power.

- Question an advertisement in the Sunday newspaper, on television, or in a catalog aimed at children: For whom is the advertisement created? Why? What does the advertiser think about boys? Girls? Families? What experiences are valued most in this text? What experiences are not included? What is this advertisement trying to do to me as a reader?

- Reread a favorite book in the classroom from a critical perspective. Why was this book a favorite? What messages is this book presenting that we hadn't considered before? If we only knew about [girls, boys, families, schools, homes, neighborhoods, life] from this book, what would we think was "true?" Why might that be a problem?

Deconstruction of Identities: Classroom Possibilities

- Particularly for students who have not experienced marginalization, it is important to deconstruct and be conscious of their privileges, and not allow their perspective to project failure onto individuals who do not "live up" to their standards. The following questions can be explored through talk, books, writing, art, or other multimedia: How does the color of your skin change how you might be treated? How does where you live affect what people think about you? How does being a boy or a girl affect the way people look at you? How does speaking a language other than English change how you are viewed by English-speaking Americans? How do your religious beliefs affect your school attendance? Follow the exploration of any of these questions with "Why do people get treated differently and why is that a problem?"

- All students can benefit from a deconstruction of their actions toward others. These actions, over time, create identities and habits of practices for ourselves that may be difficult to change. Questions to consider: How do I treat people who are different from me? Why do I treat them this way? What do I know about people who are different from me? How can I learn more? What can I do to be a person who does not judge people by their appearance? How can I become open-minded when it comes to people I don't personally know?

Reconstruction: Texts and Identities

Reconstruction is the tenet most foregrounded in Mr. Wolf's actions of writing a counterstory to the *Three Little Pigs*. Reconstruction is not always about creating new pieces of literature or written texts, it also encompasses the overt reconstruction of identities. In fictional terms, Mr. Wolf's identity may have been reconstructed through the validation of his perspective—he may come to understand himself not as a predator of innocent, cute pigs, but as a being with the right to be heard. This is farfetched, for sure, but nonetheless useful in our consideration. In our three-dimensional world stratified by class, race, gender, religion, language, sexuality, dis/ability, and so on, reconstructing identities of people who have been marginalized and devalued over the course of time is crucial in the work of critical literacy. Part of this reconstruction takes place through talk, breaking the silences that have taken up too much space in the past, and through new representations in physical texts, multimedia, and social interactions.

Reconstruction of Texts: Classroom Possibilities

- Rewrite mainstream texts from multiple perspectives, including the perspectives of students in the classroom (texts could include children's books, popular cartoons or sitcoms that students enjoy, song lyrics, advertisements for particular goods or services, etc.).

- In discussions around text, ask students if the text is like them or their family and if not, what they would change to make it more like a life they would recognize and how that would alter the messages of the text.

- Create original texts that grow from lives on the margins, suspending the concept of "taboo." These might include personal narratives, expository pieces, song lyrics, travel brochures, photographic journals, short films, newspapers, 'zines, memoirs, websites, video journals, blogs, etc.

- The reconstruction of texts is often about challenging or questioning the status quo and offering alternative perspectives on the world. Consider issues of power, perspective, and positioning in the texts that are constructed and reconstructed.

Reconstruction of Identities: Classroom Possibilities

- Locate, read, and suggest texts that productively center issues students are dealing with in their lives that are not typically in mainstream texts.[1]

- Listen intently to how students narrate themselves—or how they represent themselves through interactions with others. Recognize aspects of shame, envy, embarrassment, weakness, vulnerability, anger, etc. that can be counterproductive to personal growth and use these examples to plan future work through talk, writing, reading, or other creative constructions.

- Choose a descriptor that might be used for students in the classroom and investigate the "label." For example, what does it mean to be a girl?

A boy? Poor? White? Black? Asian? Hispanic? Rich? An English Language Learner? Mother? Father? Sibling? Learning Disabled? Handicapped? Consider the three layers of critical literacy and work with students to determine how they can be empowered by all "parts" of themselves.

● Particularly for students who have been marginalized, positioning them in the center of power relations and validating their perspectives are most important for identity reconstruction.

Social Action: Working Toward Change

Social action comes in all shapes and sizes from short-term campaigns in classrooms or schools to combat segregation (e.g., Heffernan and Lewison 2005) and to challenge mainstream children's literature to long-term inquiry and action projects around a particular social issue (e.g., Powell, Cantrell, and Adams 2001). Reconstructing powerful identities of students and families who have been stripped of dignity is social action, for sure, on a small scale affecting a small number of people. Deconstructing texts is also a form of social action, particularly when students learn to deconstruct everyday texts that attempt to persuade them to purchase goods, request services, or act in ways that won't necessarily benefit them in the long-term. For Mr. Alexander T. Wolf, the social action aspect of his tale was having a book published from his perspective, a book that will likely reach many more people than he could possibly speak to one-on-one. The social action piece of our critical literacy work in St. Francis was situated locally and focused on creating texts that centered the lives of St. Francis children and families while learning to deconstruct mainstream stories of "normal" lives. One example was highlighted in Chapter 4 and others will be highlighted in Chapters 10 and 11, but the discussion transcripts throughout the book show ways in which I privileged the lived experiences of the girls and their families through opening up such discussions and posing questions or prompts that I predicted would begin conversations around critical issues in their lives.

Social Action: Classroom Possibilities

● Photograph the school and community focusing the lens on what students both enjoy about their neighborhood and what they wish they could change. Work as a group toward desired changes.

- Launch a classroom or schoolwide campaign for working against stereo-typing people and the stereotypical representations of people in books, on television, and so on.

- Professionally publish student work that is overtly anti-racist, anti-sexist, and anti-classist and hold open houses or "galleries" to share such work with community members.

- Conduct research in the school and/or community to learn what residents view as sources of pride and what they perceive as things in need of change. Work collaboratively with community members toward change.

- After analyzing texts aimed at children as consumers such as cartoons, toy catalogs, commercials, food packaging, or fast food advertisements, write letters and persuasive essays to the creators of the texts requesting changes necessary to promote a more socially just world.

■ Layers of Critical Literacy

All texts are embedded with multiple meanings and one way to examine some of those meanings is to peel away the layers through the consideration of perspective, positioning, and power. Like the three tenets, the layers of critical literacy are never in isolation, though we may choose to foreground one over the others particularly for teaching and learning purposes. Positioning of people could not happen without someone exercising power—both power used to dominate and power used to liberate. Power, therefore, is always present in positioning and it is also always present in perspective. Mainstream perspectives become mainstream because of the way power is used by the people who hold them. Marginal perspectives, then, are pushed to the margins as a result of the lower status of the people who hold such perspectives, and in maintaining these alternative viewpoints, people continue to be positioned on the margins. These three layers, then, are always interacting with one another but there are questions we can pose to foreground one layer at a time while placing the others in the background without forgetting their existence.

Perspective

Perspective refers to the creator of the text, the text itself, and the reader. As we analyzed in Chapter 1, each person has a unique set of lived experiences that constructs what she or he assumes to be "normal." This construction of normalcy is always a fiction as it is based on understandings gained through a limited set of experiences; thus "normal" always depends upon perspective: What is normal to one person may be perceived as abnormal by another. Creators of text (spoken, written, and otherwise) are not excluded from this discussion; each speaker, writer, or composer is bound by her perspective(s) regarding the content and structure of the text and the audience for whom the text is constructed, and each of those will reflect the creator's perspective(s) on the larger society and world. Take Mr. Wolf's story, for example, by constructing a text from his perspective he has offered readers the opportunity to never "innocently" read the *Three Little Pigs* again. He has pointed out for us that the text is never simply as it lies in front of us, that there are always perspectives outside the frame that have not been included.

Perspective questions that readers can ask themselves include these:

- Who could have created this text?

- What can I guess about the perspective of the writer (composer, speaker)?

- Who are the intended audiences—how can I tell?

- What does the author think about the intended audiences?

- What readers might think the same?

- What readers might think something different?

Perspective questions that writers can ask themselves include the following:

- From what perspective am I creating this text?

- What experiences are included and why?

- What experiences are excluded and why?

- Who will my readers be and what do I think about them?

- How might a reader feel about this text if she or he has a different perspective?

- Is there a way to create this text that is inclusive of more perspectives?

Analyzing perspective and engaging *multiple perspectives* is an important part of critical literacy for both text creators (writers) and text consumers (readers[2]). The more perspectives we are able to see and understand, the more likely we will resist age-old stereotypes used to judge people, and the more likely we will recognize when we, as readers of texts, are being influenced to take on perspectives that do not align with our goals of social justice.

Positioning

Play chess? Think chess. In the first three to five moves, what pieces are in positions of vulnerability and why? Which pieces are in positions that are protected or privileged and why?

One major difference between chess pieces and real people is that chess pieces are "objects" and real people are not—we are subjects who have power to position ourselves at various times and in different contexts. *Positioning*—or the placement of someone or something by someone or something—is a post-structural concept and term that refers to the power of language and ideology that is most often visualized as a series of circles beginning with one common point and others moving out from the center (see Figure 7–3). *Center* and *margins*, two words sometimes used to analyze positioning, are perhaps easier to conceptualize within concentric circles than on a chessboard. Nevertheless, one can imagine the power and vulnerability within either metaphor. Sticking to the concentric circles, language can be used to position someone as an insider or an outsider, a winner or a loser, a good parent or a bad parent, admired or despised, in the center or on the margins—and everything that lies between such dichotomies. Because power is always shifting, positions also shift. In critical literacy, positioning, like perspective, also includes the writer (or speaker or composer, etc.), the text, and the reader.

Through decisions about what to include and exclude, structure, style, etc., the writer positions herself within the text, she may reveal bits of her history,

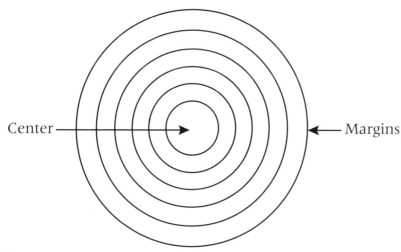

Center ——→ ←—— Margins

FIG 7–3

offer credentials or other signifying information to establish credibility to position herself as someone to whom you should listen. At other times she might position herself as someone working in solidarity with a group, or as a person with particular affinities toward various social issues. Some writers attempt to withdraw any personal identification from their texts, making it seemingly objective—yet she is still positioning herself, this time outside the words of the text, but perhaps as the truth teller, or the authority on a topic. Texts, once created by their composers, work to position readers: some readers (or listeners, or observers) will be positioned as knowers, members of the inside-joke club; others will be positioned outside the text, their perspectives, practices, and knowledge not validated in the words written and the worlds described, and others will be in between, privy to some of the knowledge that is valued in the text and not to others.

Questions a reader can ask oneself regarding *positioning*:

- Who does the writer make her/himself out to be?

- What perspectives, practices, and/or people are *centered* or valued in the text?

- What perspectives, practices, and/or people are *marginalized* or devalued in the text?

- What readers might feel like "insiders" reading this text?

- What readers might be positioned as "outsiders" by this text?

- How does this text position me?

Questions writers can ask themselves regarding *positioning*:

- How do I position myself in this text? How might my readers envision me as the writer?

- What perspectives, practices, and/or people are privileged, or centered, in my text and why?

- What am I doing to readers with perspectives similar to those in this text?

- What am I doing to readers with perspectives different from those in this text?

- Is there a way that I can write this text to make more people feel like "insiders"?

Positioning, like perspective, is not found exclusively in the literacy classroom nor in texts read and constructed in school. We position people and others position us in daily conversations; advertisements position us constantly; we position families through our lunchroom discussions, and so on. Positioning is a part of life, and working toward a critical understanding of how and why particular language practices (spoken or written) position groups of people in the *center* and on the *margins* is absolutely imperative if we are to work toward social justice as a group of educators, and work with our students to develop critical literacy practices for life.

Power

Power is always at play in human relations. Watch a small group of students gather to discuss a book they've read: how is power distributed and why? Add a teacher to the mix and what happens to the power distribution? Watch that same group travel outside to the playground and ask the same questions. Power is always *negotiated*. Think about household responsibilities and your negotiation with cohabitants (if you have any). Or consider talking with your principal about materials you want to purchase for the classroom, or your professor about a paper that is overdue. Power is never static, or stable, or still; it moves, shifts, and is used differently depending on the context in which people are relating and the people themselves. Power relations are embedded in talk, printed texts, and images.

Power can be used as a tool for domination, oppression; in other words, power can be wielded to make some people feel as if they don't have control over their present or future conditions. Power, in this sense, can be dangerous, dangerous to a democratic society, dangerous to the well-being of individual people, dangerous to the well-being of groups of people. Unchallenged use of power is particularly dangerous, as we have witnessed in historic and current events involving the attempt to obliterate specific groups of people. Genocide, as this process is often called, is a result of extreme cases of racism, classism, and discrimination grounded in gender, religion, and language that has not been systematically challenged by everyday citizens and people from outside the context of the criminal offenses. Challenging power that is intentionally used to dominate, then, is crucial in protecting the rights of individual and groups of human beings.

Resistance, then, is also powerful. Power can be used to resist domination, oppression, and other forms of dehumanization. Power can be wielded to liberate and for purposes of deconstruction, reconstruction, and social action that focuses on injustices and pursues social justice. The fact that power exists in the first place assumes that the power to resist is present. Power, then, can be used for productive purposes toward the broad goals of liberty and justice in a democratic society.

Always interrelated with positioning and perspective, uses of power *produce* the positions people might occupy and it is always determined and produced through *perspective.* Thinking critically about my own power writing this book might be helpful in this instance.

As an author, I wield much power—but not total power—over what is printed in this text. Some of the power relations I negotiate include:

- My perspectives around content (such as critical literacy) in relation to the literature already published in the field; I pay particular attention to existing publications that are of importance in the field as I attempt to work through what it is that I *want* to say, what it is that I feel I am *entitled* to say given my research and everyday experiences, and what it is that I feel I *can* or *cannot* say given the political nature of academic writing for professors. In essence, I think simultaneously about how I am positioning myself as a writer in the field of literacy and education and how I might be positioned by others inside and outside the fields.

- My perspectives around audience (such as preservice and inservice teachers) in relation to my writing style and the content I include; I constantly reflect on how this text works to position its readers, particularly aspiring teachers and teachers working with working-class and poor children and families. Careful not to position readers on the defensive, nor as occupying positions on the outside of research "knowledge," I work toward a back-and-forth dialogue between readers' experiences, my personal experiences, the research I have engaged, and literature in the field. I know that if I use my power as author in dominating ways, I may lose readers and even turn them off to concepts that I believe are very important in education. On the other hand, if I make readers too comfortable with the text, they may get the sense that they are already "doing" this sort of thing without critically reflecting on their own histories and practices in the classroom.

- My perspectives around style and content in relation to the publisher (in this case, Heinemann); This text is read critically from the publisher's perspective: audience, market, and potential sales are crucial factors in the publication process for a commercial press and these factors will sometimes alter my original intent in the writing of this book.

These are only some of the examples of power relations that I negotiate as an author, but these relations mirror those we all negotiate in everyday conversations, interactions, and engagements with reading and writing texts.

Power questions a reader can ask:

- How is the author using power in this text?

- Does the author use his or her power to repeat stereotypes or to challenge them?

- Does the author invite readers to critique the text or is the text positioned as so-called truth?

- Who, or what benefits from the power in this text?

- Who, or what would not benefit from the power in this text?

- What power relations might the author have had to negotiate through the publishing of this text?

Power questions a writer can ask:

- What power relations do I negotiate as I write this text?

- How do I use my power as author?

- Do I use my power to repeat stereotypes or challenge them? Repeat social injustices or challenge them?

- How can I make a text that doesn't claim to represent the so-called truth but acknowledges that there are multiple truths or perspectives?

Recognizing Frames

A major goal of critical literacy is the recognition that *framing* is inevitable. All texts are constructed by someone who has selected the frame that best fits her purposes and serves her interests. A critical literacy practice first focuses on this fact then moves toward deconstruction, reconstruction, and/or social action through the use of layers presented in this chapter. Critical literacy practices are often cyclical and neverending, as reconstructions are also frames chosen for particular purposes, and therefore can continue to be deconstructed. Social action, if successful, often opens up more textual representations that are in need of deconstruction and reconstruction—and yes, additional social action. Thinking and acting through the tenets and layers of critical literacy is one way educators can begin to ask the difficult questions about texts and what kinds of tools their students need to critically read their worlds.

■ Moving Beyond Framing Others: Learning About the Concrete Lives of Students

No one likes to be *framed*—we all want to be recognized as complex beings with multiple identities depending on context, with multiple talents and reasons to be valued. Framing too often leads to stereotyping, or essentializing. To not stereotype or essentialize someone, we must know her concretely, we must know some of her stories, some of her history, some of her dreams, some of her challenges. This leads us back to the importance of ethnographic research in our teaching. The only way we will be able to make informed decisions about when, how, and why to engage our students in critical literacy practices is through knowing them—well.

Chapter 8 moves back into my research with the girls, their families, and St. Francis. One of the most salient features of this research was the seeming omnipresence of the girls' mothers; mothers were often central to the girls' writing pieces, their conversations, and the prospect that mothering would be their own future became quite significant over time. The knowledge about the girls' lives and the classroom practices I share in Chapters 8 and 9 are necessarily interconnected: the more I learned, the better able I was to respond and promote critical conversations and other literacy pursuits in the classroom.

■ Notes

1   In my classroom library I had a section devoted to books and other texts that featured "tough topics to talk about." Homelessness, alcoholism, jail, and families dealing with economic deprivation were some of the topics included in the section. Though I occasionally read aloud books from this area of the library, it was used most by students during independent reading.

2   Tricky territory here, since I assume that readers are also "creators" of the texts they read; the meaning constructed from engaging with a text is unique for each reader. For simplicity's sake, however, I will leave this as is—writers intend to create a text filled with meaning and readers intend to read a text and create meaning as a result.

Relationships Outside School

8

Mothers, Daughters, and Critical Classroom Conversations

In a small-group conversation in the regular classroom, Sarah connected her perception of "mess(ing) up your life" with the lived realities of her mother. I nudged her to consider how she might make different decisions about school while being careful not to devalue the complex decisions and actions of her mother:

SARAH: You won't mess up your life by like, you won't just uh, I don't know really. You can get a house and stuff. My mom, when she was little, she wanted to help poor people.

STEPHANIE: Really? What does she say about that now?

SARAH: She says she had lots of plans like I do, but they didn't come true (Sarah's eyes dart to the floor), so she dropped out of school.

STEPHANIE: What does that make you feel like?

SARAH: That I don't wanna do that—I wanna stay in school.

STEPHANIE: Do you have lots of plans? What are your plans?

SARAH: Yeah, I want to be a writer, or a nurse, or a psychologist.

STEPHANIE: If you have all these big plans, what are you going to do to make those plans come true?

SARAH: Try to remember 'em when I get older, like when I'm a teenager. And say, "I gotta stay in school. I gotta take a chance."

Now hear the voices of mothers as they articulate a deep hope and desire for their girls to grow into "somebody," to be "successful," and to "achieve" something that has eluded the mothers themselves:

She's gonna be somebody. She is. She is gonna be something. And I can see it now.

—Cadence's Mother

I think Joanie will stay in school. [She] seen how we struggle. She is so intelligent. I think she could be a lawyer or doctor or somethin'.

—Joanie's Mother

I'm hopin' and prayin' for her. She has so much hope and enthusiasm. I want her to be somebody.

—Faith's Mother

I want her to stay in school for one, and be where she'll be happy.

—Rose's Mother

I wanna see her do her best and achieve whatever goals she sets up to do. Achieve—be successful, not cleaning toilets. We don't want [her] to struggle like we do.

—Callie's Mother

Don't be a young mom. Wait. Be successful.

—Heather's Mother

Urging their daughters to wait to have children, to "be successful," to "be somebody," these mothers echo a long tradition of working-class and poor families hoping that their children will take a different path than they themselves had (Finders 1997; hooks 1996; Luttrell 1997; MacLeod 1995; Santiago 1993; Sennett and Cobb 1972; Walkerdine, Lucey, and Melody 2001). Such aspirations, both on the part of caregivers and children, are much more complex than we tend to seriously consider since becoming someone different from one's mother or father often means becoming like someone who wasn't necessarily respected or trusted by the family. Sennett and Cobb (1972) write about a forty-four-year-old man who feels "threatened by his children, who are 'turning out just the way I want them to be'" (19). Some of these complexities and contradictions will be explored in the rest of this chapter as I present a number of transcripts from conversations held with the girls both inside the regular classroom and in the afterschool program. Excerpts from conversations with mothers will also be included, but the focus will be on the young girls' perceptions of what it means to be a girl in St. Francis, my own autobiographical narratives around mother-daughter relations, and discussions of how some girls' decision making might be wrapped up in what I call *answerability* to their mothers, or their sense of responsibility owed to them and their lives.

These discussions will come together to help us think about how identities assembled around mothering might impact one's future and aspirations.

Seven of the girls in this study lived intense, close relationships with their mothers. The girls' mothers and their relationships with their daughters were represented in the classroom and in the afterschool program through informal conversations, responses to books and films, in their informal writing (such as in writer's notebooks), and in formal, more public writing such as pieces that were shared with classmates or even "published" to be placed in the classroom library, on display in the school, or within texts that were distributed outside of school (one example being Chapter 11). The ever-present nature of mothers and grandmothers throughout the study prompted me to build upon conversations about mothers and mothering, and engaging the girls in critical explorations of the gendered nature of such work. Contemplating the multiple ways these students were creating their "selves" within their relationships with their mothers, I was able to analyze how such identities might impact the girls' engagements with schooling and consider what that might mean for school and classroom practices.

Mothering Identities

I am most passionate in my relationship with mama. It is with her that I feel loved and sometimes accepted. She is the one person who looks into my heart, sees its needs and tries to satisfy them. . . . The fact that I disappoint her leaves me lying awake at night sobbing, wanting to be a better daughter, a daughter that makes her life brighter, easier . . . I want so much to please her and yet keep some part of me that is myself, my own. . . .

—bell hooks (1996, 139–140)

The only person I need to answer to is my Mama and God. And I'm an adult, so I can give [mama] the wrong answer.

—Lori, mother of Cadence

There is a tiny black-and-white photograph of me as a one-year-old in the newspaper. I am accompanied by four generations of women: my mother, her mother, her mother, and her mother. Four mothers and a baby—four mothers and a future mother. The image is clear and strong within the pages of my baby book created by my mother. I was the firstborn of the fifth living generation in 1971 and it was a celebration of a long line of strong, mothering women—the only people I needed to answer to. My daughter Hayden has a similar picture: On the day of her birth she lay swaddled in my arms with my mother and grandmother hovering. Three mothers and a baby—three mothers and a future mother. The image will likely be as clear and strong to Hayden as it was to me growing up. The women in my photograph turned out to be extended caretakers of my brother, sister, and me, but there were others involved as well. Our girl cousins, some as young as eleven and twelve, carried us around, bought toys for us, played games with us, took us to boyfriends' homes, fed us, clothed us, played house with us. They were clearly mothers already—we were merely props in their performances. Aunts and great aunts were always there too. Aunt Norma, my mother's only sister, chose to remain in the mountains of Kentucky. I stayed with her for days at a time; my brother sometimes stayed the entire summer. Aunt Karen, my mother's closest childhood friend with no biological relation, was another caretaker, and her daughter taught me some important skills I learned as a young girl coming of age, namely street fighting, cussing, and smoking.

My mothering identity, constructed within working-poor gender-specific relations, began quite young and has thickened over time. This part of my self, the self that answers (in a broad sense) to my mother and the maternal lineage while caring for others, is not only important to me, but has dominated much of my psyche. The *answerability*[1] and responsibility of my daily activities, dialogue, and future plans are often reflective of my moral commitment to my mother, even when she is not physically present. Major decisions about where to go to school, where to live, how to rear my daughter, and how to structure my routine life are all parts of constructing identities and have been negotiated between different selves—with the self acting in response to my mother typically carrying more weight. I have made these decisions based on a conscious *answering* to my mother and the particularities of her life.

◼ Why Does This Matter?

As educators, understanding the complexities of familial relationships in working-poor communities such as St. Francis is critical for recognizing the pain and ambiguity young students may face as they make academic and potentially life-altering decisions. The idea that a *thickening* identity of mothering begins very young for the girls in St. Francis and this caretaking construct might lead girls to make what they may perceive as decisions between "school" and "family" is complicated. Comprehending the enormity of these conditions is critical for teachers to begin constructing positive, fruitful relationships with mothers and their daughters in an effort to help students create more hybrid identities that don't shed family commitments but instead incorporate academic achievement and an ability to enter a more economically stable life.

In the following section, young girls narrate ideas of being a girl, growing into a woman, and the complexities of such positions. Their dialogue is responsive (and what I'm calling answerable) not only to one another and to me as leader of the group, but also to others who aren't present: their mothers.

■ Early Stages of a Mothering Identity

Beginning in November of their second-grade year, the girls and I met after school one day each week. On a cool crisp Tuesday afternoon we greeted one another while eating our snack—bananas, warm chocolate chip cookies, and cashews on this particular day—and I opened up a conversation about what it means to be a girl, and then what it's like for a girl when she grows into a woman. The discussion moved instantly into one of *mothering*: caring for children, experiencing trouble with men, tending to household duties, and working to provide for the family. These young girls held great insights about womanhood in St. Francis and even went so far as to consider themselves *mothers*.

"What do you think it's like for a girl when she grows up?" I asked the girls as we sit on the floor in a circle with our writing notebooks placed in front of us.

"Keep a secret from boys," Rose responded quickly.

"It's hard," Cadence smirked.

"What do you mean 'hard'?" I probed.

"Because it's hard work—and we have a house and people be living with us, and there're boys, like our brothers and stuff, they'll be like messin' up the house and stuff and. . . ."

Heather interrupts, "And if they mess up the house they'll tell that we're doin' it!"

Rose and Cadence were speaking about an adult woman's life as they imagine it, as they've witnessed it. Heather's interruption carried the conversation in a different direction, one rooted in her own experiences as a young girl, not her experiences of analyzing her mother's position. The other girls did not continue the route Heather opened up to them, instead they pursued the roles they've watched women take on and the messiness of it all. The conversation continued when someone suggested that a *dude* might leave the mom:

"Yeah, cuz then you'll have to hire somebody to babysit *her* and I couldn't trust nobody with my baby," Callie told the group.

Cadence added, "I won't trust nobody with mine."

"What do you think it's like to be your mom? All of your moms are women. What do you think it's like to be your mom?" I asked the group.

Joanie leaned forward and began, "It's like. . . ."

"It's *bor*ing," replied Alexis, rolling her eyes.

Joanie tried again, "It is—they get like—my mom gets in lots of trouble. Like, my dad is always mad and he does stuff and then my mom just gets mad and. . . ."

"I think it's fun to be a mom 'cuz you get to love your children. And you get to love your family," Heather inserted, cutting Joanie's comment short.

Cadence added, "I wanna be a mom because—because my mom is special because we can't have a job, so I wanna job."

"It's hard because sometimes our parents get in fights and it's hard trouble for them to work it out," reported Callie.

"I like being a mom, " Rose stated quietly with wide eyes.

■ Already Mothers?

Rose, an eight-year-old girl during this conversation, reported quietly and simply, "I like being a mom." She wasn't the only one in this group who demonstrated a slip of consciousness and a linguistic move that traveled directly into her hypothetical future as a mother. Callie told us emphatically, "I couldn't trust nobody with my baby." Cadence empathized with Callie's dilemma and asserted with a strong voice, "I *won't* trust nobody with mine."

A girl growing up in St. Francis is a woman with a baby. This future is clear and unchallenged throughout the conversations with the girls. Over time, however, some challenges were asserted when Heather, whose mother had just given birth to a child and was having a great deal of difficulty with child care and job demands, said, "I ain't having kids." This type of opposition to bearing children was rare. The girls spoke not only about their mothers and their desire to be their mothers, but they also acted in stereotypical motherly ways—caring for younger siblings, cousins, and neighbors.

In her analysis of nineteenth-century writing by young girls living in poverty in Britain, Steedman (1982) writes of the early development of little girls' identities as mothers. In their free time away from work, young girls were playing with miniature furniture, toy cutlery, and so on, but they did not own a doll: "She did not need to play at being a mother in order to assimilate that role, for, in fact, to all intents and purposes she and other girls like her *were* mothers, did not play *at* having babies, but played with them" (123). Though times have changed slightly and the probability of a very young girl being left alone to care for a baby has lessened, this felt experience of being a caretaker was demonstrated by the girls in Steedman's study in the 1970s. Here, in the new millennium, young daughters living in poverty in the United States continue the narration of not *pretending* to be, but *being* mothers with minimal consideration of self-fulfillment in other ways. In the next several sections, we will see that these gendered and classed identities grow largely out from, into, and through the mother-daughter bond.

■ Daughters of Young Working Mothers

Every mother of the eight major participants in this study gave birth to her first child in her teen years, some as early as fifteen years of age and others as late as eighteen. This teen-mothering trend is commonplace for young girls living in St. Francis, and it isn't slowing in the present time in other working-class or poor neighborhoods in the United States (DeParle 2004; Edin and Kefalas 2005), nor—contrary to popular belief—has it increased in recent history (Luttrell 2003). Early experimentation with heterosexuality, coupled with a thickening identity of a "mother," alongside trouble with an authoritarian school system that ignores gendered and classed lives can be a recipe for young motherhood (see Luttrell 1997, 2003). Though each mother in this study proclaimed they "wouldn't give nothing for my kids," each also urged her young daughter(s) to "wait to have kids."

Callie's mother (Bonnie) surprised me one day as I sat in her living room, all her children within hearing distance in the kitchen, when she started a lively conversation about the sex education program at Bruger Elementary School. Her oldest daughter was entering high school, "the same age I was when I had my oldest," she told me with a worried look. Bonnie was not only concerned about her daughters being sexually active, but she was also terrified they would become pregnant and not finish high school. Her fear was common among all the mothers. Bonnie and the others had learned the difficult lessons of trying to raise children under material conditions afforded by poverty and they truly believed that receiving a high school diploma would change the possible futures of their children. Regardless of their potential for contributing to society at large, these mothers placed their mothering duties first and foremost in their minds, as well as in their physical work. These duties, for a working-poor mother, nearly engulfed any possibility of continuing education in order to gain entrance into a higher-paying position; as Cadence's mom (Lori) told me, "I'm afraid to start [nursing school] and have to stop because of the hardships."

Instead, these women made their living in low-wage labor positions: nursing home aides, industrial cleaning, aides in schools, and fast-food service. One mother worked part-time as a homework helper at the local girls and boys club and one mother's employment was inconsistent at best, as she was battling an alcohol problem. The only mother who had her foot in the door of an institution that may lead to an easier material life was also the only mother who had *any* post-secondary education: Dena (Heather's mom). Dena worked in the securities department for a local bank, but during the summer following Heather's fourth-grade year she began working a second job (in retail) to help make ends meet. Even entry-level professional work could not sustain the family of four. Seven of the eight mothers worked full-time, and some worked more than one full-time job, including the only mother without a long-term stable live-in partner (Lori). Though there were periods between jobs when a mother had been fired due to absenteeism or tardiness—which was more often than not a result of mothering duties—seven of the eight mothers in this study worked regularly. Their long, hard, laborious hours of work, however, were not enough to ease their economic woes. All of them relied on federal assistance (food stamps, healthcare, housing subsidies, and/or cash) to some degree, and seven of them had a long-term male partner who was also working—some gained access to goods or money through the informal economy[2] including under-the-table handyman work, bartering, or the illegal economies of drug trafficking and buying and selling stolen property.

The hardships that come along with rearing children under such conditions can be daunting, even for a two-parent household. Delaying motherhood and working toward powerfully positioning oneself in the twenty-first century workplace would be ideal according to many mothers in St. Francis. Deciding to do this can be extremely difficult, however, when you begin practicing, idolizing, and desiring motherhood by age six. Over time this thickening identity of oneself *as* a mother may ache to be fulfilled. And even if a young girl does make the decision to put off motherhood and position herself differently (than her mother) in the marketplace—this decision may be perceived as the ultimate betrayal and the opposite of answerability: the betrayal of an identity formed within the intimately psychological, social, and cultural mother-daughter bond.

■ The Desire to Mother: Working, Caring, Arguing, and Dreaming

Cadence, a girl with an olive complexion and deep green eyes, wished to be her mother. The role that she wanted to fill wasn't necessarily one of caretaking, but instead one of providing. Cadence's mom, Lori, was the only lone parent within this project and she always worked at least one full-time job and one part-time job to get closer to paying the monthly bills. Cadence did not wish to be *a* mother, but *her* mother. As I stood up to leave Cadence's grandpa's compact two-bedroom apartment that was serving as home for Lori and her three girls, Lori pulled her hair up into a bun, put her lunch and book in a backpack and headed out the door to walk to her third-shift position at a local nursing home. She looked at me hard in the eyes and said, "I work— that's what I do." Cadence also wanted to work, to be the providing mother that must find a babysitter so that she *can* work. In two separate entries in her writer's notebook during second grade, Cadence wrote:

> I wish that I could be my mom because she gets jobs and I don't get a job. I wish that I could too, but my mom won't let me.

> When I grow up I will have some children. I will have to get a babysitter.

Much like Cadence, Heather wanted to be *her* mother and she often said things that pointed to the caretaking of children versus the material providing role Cadence focused on, saying things like, "I wish I can be my mom because you get to love your kids." With the recent addition of a baby brother, Heather was nearly obsessed with caring for others, thinking of having children, and being a mother despite her own mother's urgings to "wait to have kids." Heather adored her mother and wrote about her often. Heather plays the mother role as she cares for her baby brother in the following story:

> Dear writer's notebook, I have a new baby brother. He is beautiful. He looks like me. His name is Jed. He was named after my dad. I can hold him and I can feed him. I can push him in the stroller. I can make him smile. When he grows up I am getting him a car. I like to sleep by him. When he cries I can stop him and sometimes he can sleep with me in my bed. When I get home I am going to give him a bath and take him outside with me. I am taking him to the park and having a picnic and then I am going to show him off. I love my brother.
> —Heather, second grade

Like most of the young girls in this community, Heather was already attuned to many of the details of caring for babies. Her seven-year-old hip swung to the side and she propped Jed on it as if she was a mature grandmother that had been doing this sort of thing for years. Sarah had also become a big sister and she described step-by-step how to make a bottle for her newborn sister. From the measuring of formula to checking the temperature, it was clear that Sarah had performed this task many times and felt quite comfortable—even expected—to do so.

All eight of the girls demonstrated detailed knowledge and understanding about what it takes to mother children that echoed themes of responsibility, power, and independence that is often ignored by school authorities (Finders 1997; Luttrell 1997). In a conversation during the beginning of their third-grade year, the girls began discussing their impatience in growing up, which led immediately—*again*—to mothering responsibilities.

■ Kids, Boyfriends, Marriages

Rose stated, "I can't wait to grow up."

"I never wanna grow up," Joanie responded.

"I'm gonna have kids," Callie added, smiling.

"I'm gonna have a boyfriend," Joanie decided.

"Get married. . . ," Callie interjected.

"When I'm eighteen," Joanie added.

The girls began to talk about all the wonderful things one does when she has children—decorating shoeboxes, buying clothes and hair accessories, getting a hair cut, purchasing brand new shoes, playing in the snow, taking dogs outside. Their conversation was full of bliss and excitement. I felt obliged to ask them about another side of mothering.

"It sounds like everything you're describing is so wonderful. Are there some things about having kids that might not be so great?" I asked.

"Yeah!" yelled Heather.

"Whatever *goes* around *comes* around," Callie told us quickly.

I asked, "What do you mean?"

"Your kids will be like you," she responded with a smirk.

"But they cry all the time," Joanie told us.

Callie continued, "When you grow up and have kids, they'll just be like you."

"It makes more people in the world," Joanie reminded us happily.

"It makes more workers in the world," Heather added.

"And then they—like—what school you went to, probly *they'll* go to. They'll be greedy like you, picky like you," Callie recalled the familiar theme of how kids become just like their mothers (in this case).

Heather snapped, "I'm not picky!"

Joanie admitted, "I'm the picky one."

"They'll be grouchy all the time," Callie continued her theme.

"Like me," reported Joanie.

"Be grouchy about school—'I hate school, I hate that, I hate this'," Callie went on.

Callie's insight that "your kids will be like you" is one that may have been initiated through narratives in her home. Stories her mother might have told Callie to convince her to behave in different, less confrontational ways. These narratives were now finding their way into Callie's own repertoire. The idea that "your kids will be like you" assumes there will be kids, this is left unstated, but the fact that children will exhibit the same hard-to-deal-with characteristics of being grouchy, complaining, and being picky is articulated by Callie and is agreeable among most of the other girls. Later in the conversation, however, Callie inserted another narrative likely heard first in her home and later taken on as her own story. The notion of wanting one's child to have a *different* kind of childhood is a theme that ran throughout the mothers' stories, but was only first represented within the girls' stories in the beginning of third grade.

■ I Want Them to Grow Up Different

Callie told the group, "When you have 'em [kids] they'll be grouchy like you and I don't want them to be growin' up like *me*. I want them to grow up *different*."

"Like what?" I asked.

"Like how *they* wanna be—not how *I* wanna be—or how their dad wants them to be."

"Tell us about that—I don't know what you mean," I probe.

"They wanna do what they wanna do—they don't wanna do what we did," Callie adds.

Desiring a childhood for one's daughter that is less stressful, filled with less tension and responsibility, and overall just a bit easier was commonly discussed by all the mothers. Within one very short conversation Callie had articulated the tricky web of hopes, desires, and fears among mothers and daughters. The desire to have a child be *just like* you—yet the *fear* that she *will* be just like you, and "pay you back" for what you did to your own mother is a complicated contradiction of emotions and hopes. Callie also described the expectation that children would attend the same elementary school as the mother, but then later added the hope, or fantasy, that a daughter's life will be *different* from the mother's—that the daughter will make her own choices and not be bound by the life course of the mother. This contradiction reveals yet more challenges facing young girls in St. Francis. The assumed course (largely unstated, but implied by Callie here) of life is that of the mother's. The *desired* outcome, however, is quite different—that the daughter will make decisions that are best for her without considering what it was that her mother did before her.

Though Callie and the other girls were likely to hear similar narratives told by their mothers at home—narratives with themes of autonomous decision making and life-altering decisions (staying in school versus dropping out)— Callie had *already*, at the age of eight, decided that these were *her* narratives. She was already desiring that *her* child live a different childhood from herself and that *her* child will have the opportunity to make decisions on her own without feeling obligated to follow in the footsteps of the mother (Callie) or an unnamed father. In this narration, Callie had made the decision to live the life course of her own mother and was now articulating her dreams for a child who had not been realized in the physical sense—but had certainly been realized in some sense. Callie's depiction of her certain (in her eyes at this point) future was one that was woven throughout the intergenerational lives of young girls and women in St. Francis. Choosing to do something *different* from that of her mother, a daughter could be perceived as defying a long line of strong, hard-working women who have built their lives around the caring and providing for others in a working-poor material life. This long line of women had set aside aspirations for themselves outside of mothering (in a broad sense) and work day and night to ensure physical and emotional safety for those within their care.

Exercise 8.1 Negotiating Family Relations and Academic Success

Working-class and poor parents often suggest they want their daughter to "do better" than they, and in this chapter Callie even implied this as a goal for *her* future children. Parents want their daughter to achieve the American Dream that has slipped away from their generation; they want her to *change* her class status. To say this, in some way, is to downgrade the work and life that these parents have lived. For a girl to choose a *different* way of life, perhaps a life gained through academic achievement, she could be perceived as devaluing the paths her parents have taken.

This complicated situation makes academic success contradictory for many girls. These conflicts can be so great that girls disconnect from school and find themselves in a world of low-wage labor that perpetuates cycles of working poverty. In contrast to the deficit theories available to explain the continual cycle of academic failure and poverty among poor Whites, I argue that for these groups of students, academic success can bring much contradiction and turmoil, and perhaps a deep ethical and moral commitment to one's family history and relationships plays more of a role than any supposed "deficiencies" of working-class and poor children. Walkerdine, Lucey, and Melody (2001) state:

> First and foremost we argue that for all working-class young women, the fact that they are engaged in a process of transformation, of becoming different from their families . . . impacts powerfully on their conscious and unconscious lives. In this psychosocial landscape educational success can bring as many fears and anxieties as failure. (142)

Walkerdine grew up in a working-class family and writes about her experiences crossing social class lines between home and school. This crossing over implied a different set of values, practices, and perceptions of the world. "When some of us went to school, especially to grammar schools, we learned very quickly to split off home from school, to see our families as ignorant, our culture was stupid" (1998, 96).

With this commentary in mind, respond to the following prompts and questions:

● Did you ever experience what Walkerdine explains as splitting "off home from school"?

● If you are from a working-class or poor background, talk or write about your experiences of striving to "do better" than your caretakers. Were you always motivated? If so, what motivated you? If not, what complications played a role in your upward mobility?

● If you are not from a working-class or poor background, talk or write about your experiences between home and school. Did you feel comfortable in school? Was your family comfortable or confident interacting with teachers and administrators? How did these experiences shape your understandings about school and academic achievement?

As an elementary teacher I always believed that building genuine, lasting relationships with students from working-class and poor backgrounds would help ease the contradictions they faced between school, home, and attempting to achieve more academically than the generations before them. I suppose the progressive movement in education promoted such relationships and my own fond memories of Ms. Stritt and one or two others led me to conclude that relationships were at the core of *my* feeling connected to school in any real way at all. In fact, at the very point when I felt least connected to my teachers, the downward spiral began that would nearly end my hopes of being the first in my family to graduate from high school.

Relationship building, however, is not the silver bullet we all hope for. This study forced me to critically reconsider the power of relationships between young girl students and their White, middle-class female teachers. Like many elementary teachers, it was noted that I could "connect" well with students, that students "loved" me, and that students "talked about" me all the time. It never occurred to me that such a bond in the classroom could position a child awkwardly at home.

This chapter has set the stage for understanding the potential conflict between a White, middle-class female teacher and a working-class or poor mother of any ethnicity by looking at why and how the young girls in this study were faithful to their mothers in many ways, including stories about their own futures that would mirror their mothers' lives. Chapter 9 will highlight such conflict and consider it through three layers of critical literacy: perspective, positioning, and power.

■ Notes

1   This is a concept and term from the work of moral philosopher Mikhail Bakhtin used to theorize ethical relations between the self and the other. I take liberty here in my use of this term as I include an "other" in the conversation who is not physically present: the girls' mothers. I argue that their moral commitment to the absent other and the experiences they've had with that person (their mothers) informs their interactions in school and with me during out-of-school activities.

2   See Halperin (1998) for a discussion on the informal economy in working-class communities and hooks (2000) for a discussion on the illegal trade as the only booming economy in poor communities and the social, emotional, and political effects of such.

Relationships Inside School

Teacher as Potential Threat

9

R elationship building between students and teachers is often emphasized in teacher education programs, professional development, and within individual school cultures through leadership initiatives around community building. I, too, once believed that relationships with students that were built on mutual respect and understanding were an imperative piece in not only "effective" education, but transformational education. I wasn't astute enough to realize that students, or the girls in this case, are *not* free to attach themselves to whomever they wish—they are girls who have already constructed themselves as similar in many ways to their mothers, and in many ways *answerable to* their mothers. Thus their attachment to me, in order to be productive and sustaining, must also be perceived by them as answerable to their mother. The first clue I had that this was not the case was a journal entry by Faith:

> Mom,
>
> I like girls group because Mrs. Jones is nice to me. I don't know why she is, maybe she's trying to be nice. But I care about you mom. Okay? I'm trying to be nice.
>
> —Faith, spring of second grade

When I discovered this entry I just stared at it—my heart sinking into my big toe.

Of course.

Duh.

The lightbulb went off in my head. Who did I think I was? Faith's entry is one that can be read as a dialogue that had played out at her home, or at least a hypothetical discussion Faith imagined having with her mother. Faith's mom wanted to know why I was being so *nice* and Faith wanted to reassure her mother that *she* is the one Faith cares about and she is simply "trying to be nice" to me. The suspicion. The fear. A stereotyped middle-class other (me) who was feared and not trusted had now become a particular someone. A concrete person who is perceived to have the same power as the institution (school), *and* is making a move toward the private sphere of the family. A concrete other who seems to care for, nurture, and teach a woman's little girl. An intruder not only into the goings-on of family life, but a White, middle-class woman who is gaining the respect of a young daughter of an African American mother who had recently been homeless and barely able to provide food for her family.

When I visited Faith's home I sensed the discomfort of her mother, Chestina, as she sat a safe distance away from me on the couch. Chestina watched me speak as if she was waiting for an accusation. I felt defensive, even intimidated by her stare, and in those moments my Whiteness and my Middle Classness couldn't have been more painfully obvious. Though time helped soothe our tensions and we gradually built a friendly acquaintanceship, Chestina sometimes chose not to be at home when I had scheduled a visit. Instead, her husband (Faith's father) would be there waiting anxiously to tell me how he felt Faith was doing in school and what he would change about school if he had the power to do so.

Perplexed by my perception that Chestina didn't trust me, I decided to open up the conversation with another mother in the study, Lori, who seemed comfortable with me and after a couple years even began to initiate visits. Without mentioning names, I asked Lori for advice after describing the discomfort between Faith's mother and myself. Lori told me blatantly, "I didn't trust you at first." As Lori continued, she seemed more fidgety than usual, making me fidgety too. Lori told me that she thought Cadence "had a good family life" and she thought that she was "a good mother." Lori later implied that perhaps some mothers (but not *she*) were uncomfortable with me because I was offering their daughters something that the mother was unable to provide: "Somethin' they're not gettin' at home." Lori's advice to me was to continue talking to Chestina and slowly help her to feel more at ease with my relationship with Faith.

The idea that Lori would suggest that I, a White, middle-class female school teacher, would have something to offer girls that their working-poor mothers could not echoes the rhetoric of the "ideal mother." The White, middle-class mother has been constructed as the ideal mother who turns work into play, disciplines using nurturing strategies of progressive classrooms, negotiates rules with children, and uses social networks to ensure her child's success in school and life in general. Though literature has criticized the raised (and impossible) demands of middle-class mothers who attempt to reach the pinnacle of the ideal mother (Lareau 2000; Reay 1998; Walkerdine, Lucey, and Melody 2001), the standard is still set. And though it is permeable and changes with time and place, standards for reaching ideal motherhood are always based on the economic, social, and cultural resources of the White middle-class (Collins 1994; Luttrell 1997; Rich 1981; Walkerdine, Lucey, and Melody, 2001). Walkerdine and colleagues (2001) write:

> Texts on education are constantly full of the need to make parents responsible for getting it right for their children from infancy onwards. Women therefore bear an incredible burden and responsibility and we argue that it is middle-class women who are understood as the purveyors of normality and have to be strictly regulated, and indeed to regulate themselves. . . . By contrast working-class women demonstrate a number of tendencies in their child-rearing practices that are considered abnormal. This means that they have to be policed by educational, social welfare and medical agencies (indeed middle-class women) because they tend to utilize strategies of child rearing that have far stronger boundaries between work and play, make power differentials clear and do not value rationality at the expense of other ways of being. It is these women who for many decades have been held responsible for the educational failure of their children. (114)

Lori has internalized at least pieces of this argument, that middle-class mothers mother in "normal" ways. Therefore, Lori envisions me as someone who might fit the category of "ideal mother," having something to offer the girls that their mothers cannot offer. She suggested this as one possible reason why Faith's mother didn't trust me, but I want to argue that in some way, Lori also perceives me as an ideal mother who offers her daughter something she cannot. This position, the enduring tensions between mother and middle-class teacher, presents a threat to the mother-daughter relationship discussed in Chapter 8. This threat can be either indirect (as in the case of Faith's mother questioning my intentions) or quite direct, as discussed in the following scenario.

More than two years after I met Lori, I was sitting in the kitchen of her newly leased-to-own home. I had stopped by in sweatpants and ponytail to drop off the transcripts of our latest interview and sat down to briefly discuss them. Somehow (I forget, really) the topic of Child Protective Services was raised and I got quite a surprise. Until this point I thought that Lori's family was the only one untouched in the study by the fear and intervention of 888-KIDS (the well-known phone number for the local Child Protective Services). Unbeknownst to me, and likely consciously withheld by Lori in the past, Cadence and her two older sisters had been in foster care two separate times, initiated by reports to 888-KIDS. The story came pouring out of Lori, who paused only to dab at her watering eyes and yell at her girls to stay in the other room.

When Cadence was two years old, she and her sisters were attending a "highfalutin" daycare facility behind a private school just north of their neighborhood. Lori was single and working two full-time jobs and thrilled to have such a nice caretaking arrangement for her daughters. Two weeks after her girls were there, the daycare provider called requesting that Lori pick them up and keep them home for a week because the girls had carried lice into the facility and they were wearing "dirty clothes." When the girls returned after a week, a caretaker noticed a bruise on one of them and reported Lori to 888-KIDS.

"Social services came in the house and saw dog poop. The court took the kids. Cadence was only two years old. They said, 'You don't have clean clothes and your house is filthy,'" Lori told me, recalling exact dates of events that occurred more than five years earlier. The girls were taken from their home on November 27 and Lori wasn't allowed to see them for a week. It took three days for her to get someone to tell her where they were. After a week she received supervised visits that occurred once a week for two hours. Lori told me, "They saw dirty clothes on the floor in a basket, dishes in the sink, and food on the counter. They saw stains on the carpet. I said, 'I work two jobs!'"

The court ordered her to quit one of those jobs. "You can't work all those hours," they told her. Lori lost one job because of the ordeal, which caused her to miss work, so the court's wish was granted. Lori moved, got rid of her dog, and for the next two weeks received at-home supervised visits with the girls. Lori described the frustration and violation she had felt, "Fuck you, you can't tell me how to raise these kids!" she reported telling the judge. His response, in her words, was, "We have *evidence* of filth!" All along the girls had been separated. Cadence and the middle daughter were in one home and the oldest daughter was in a separate home. After weeks of begging, Lori's request for the three girls to be together was granted. Finally, after Christmas, the girls were returned to their home with Lori and received regular home visits from social service workers for six months.

"And this is how we fell into this thing," she tells me—setting me up for a clear discussion of tensions between middle-class and working-class and poor women and idealized versions of mothering.

Months after the initial encounter with child protection services, 888-KIDS was called by a neighbor who reported the girls being home alone. The oldest was in third grade and Cadence, the youngest, was a little over three years old.

Lori was working a split shift at the nursing home and had an ongoing babysitting arrangement with her mother who lived less than a three-minute walk away. On this particular day, Lori's mother didn't think she had to go back to work in the afternoon and when Lori called to tell her mother she was walking out the door, the answering machine clicked on. Assuming that her mother was in the restroom, temporarily busy around the house, or already walking to get the kids, Lori left a message that she was leaving the house. Her mother didn't get the message, however, until she got home from Bingo that evening—and by that time it was too late.

"They had a very nice foster mother. She bought them new clothes and everything. She was single and lived in a beautiful mansion. They had all the brand new things that I couldn't give them. Cadence didn't want to come with me." This broke Lori's heart and she began to cry. Tears welled in my eyes too, as I sat and listened to the painful recounting. After months of their living with Janeene (the foster mother), Lori finally got custody of the girls. On Janeene's request, the court ordered supervised visits for Janeene and the girls, and eventually Janeene petitioned the court for full custody of the girls: she wanted to adopt them.

In Lori's words, Janeene's argument was, "I can provide *all* this. What can *she* provide?" And her hypothetical response was, "I'm their *mother*. I can provide more than you!" But this confidence eluded Lori during the struggle for her children and she told me, "I thought it was better for them. I thought I was worthless. I had a three-room apartment—she had a big mansion. They had their own bedrooms." She had considered giving them up, believing that material goods and a middle-class existence would be better for them. But she couldn't follow through with it and fought Janeene in court:

"I was so ready to go kidnap and snatch them. I had money ready and everything. I'm poor, you know, lower class. Not rich—not even middle class. Desperate times call for desperate measures. I'm glad I had the fire." Janeene began visiting with Lori one-on-one and once they became acquainted, Janeene dropped her pursuit of the girls. Once she came to know Lori and saw her interact with the girls, she couldn't imagine disrupting the family again.

"She did care for my kids, I respect her for that," Lori tells me. "But still today, my children will not be around another female."

There is a clear and direct connection in Lori's story between the harsh judgments of the "highfalutin" child care providers at school, 888-KIDS, foster care, and the real threat of losing one's children to a White, middle-class woman who can provide material goods, space, and experiences that a working-poor mother simply can't. Like the writings of Walkerdine, Lucey, and Melody (2001), Lori's story is embedded with the policing of working-class (poor) mothers by middle-class women, and the experienced justification of an ongoing fear of institutional workers. Even Lori told me, "I live in constant fear of 888-KIDS." Lori perceived White, middle-class women who build relationships with her daughters to be a real threat not only to the mother-daughter bond, but also to the family structure as a whole. "My children will not be around another female," is a strong statement reflecting her perceptions of threat and clarifies why Lori told me that at first she "didn't trust" me either: thus the inconspicuous location of the well-intentioned White, middle-class, female primary school teacher.

■ Rethinking Relationships

Thus far I have attempted to demonstrate the need for another level of understanding of students' lives. Students who walk into classrooms do not possess autonomy to build relationships and attachments with *any* concrete other. The decisions for doing so may result in tensions at home, as in the cases of Faith and Cadence. Mothers may sense a threat when someone from the institution—who is respected on many levels—begins building relationships with their daughters. Implicit throughout Lori's narrative is a theme of inferiority, even contemplating giving up her children due to her perception that the superior social class standing of a woman would be "better" for her kids. But now Lori vows to never let this sort of relationship between another woman and her daughters build again, and she doesn't allow her girls to be alone with "another female."

Families in this study recognized institutions as arms of the state and feared them just as they often ridiculed them. This ongoing preoccupation is detrimental in the educational experiences of children and families and unproductive for teachers and school authorities who work to transform systemic inequities. Lareau writes about parents and teachers as "natural enemies" due to parents' particular concerns around one child and teachers' universalistic concerns for all the children (170). I want to argue that parents and teachers are not "natural" enemies, but instead each group has been constructed as an other who is not to be completely respected or trusted. These constructions are socially produced, and therefore can be deconstructed and reconstructed across time. With this in mind, I began working as a teacher-researcher to dismantle the carefully assembled barriers between institutional workers and the residents of St. Francis. Building genuine relationships with the young girls is where I began, often sharing my personal history as a girl growing up working-poor. This relationship building, however, created new complications that I had not consciously considered as a former classroom teacher or as an activist ethnographer focused on class relations.

The relationships educators build with children may continue to position them in tension-filled spaces between home and school if we don't realize the necessity of building genuine relationships with caregivers as well. This kind of work is long-term and can be tiring. It also requires the support of schools for teachers to engage with parents in the neighborhood, and in their homes over longer stretches of time—the work of teacher-ethnographers. Faith's journal entry and Lori's story about 888-KIDS didn't surface for two years, and I would have never known about either had I engaged with the family for the traditional one year, set as standard in most schools. Consciously deconstructing myself as the ideal mother with the perfect life (insinuated by the girls and their mothers from time to time) made most of the mothers more comfortable with me, leading to richer conversations that helped me understand their situated lives more clearly—but this didn't happen overnight.

Exercise 9.1 Becoming Concrete to Families— and Seeing Families in Concrete Ways

One of the enduring tensions between school authorities and families is the persistent "us" and "them" mentality. An important first step in lessening such tensions and building genuine partnerships doesn't lie in more parent-education classes, workshops, etc. that so many districts offer, but in *dialogue*—real discussions between teachers and caretakers, between administrators and community members, and between children and school authorities. Consider the following table as a framework for discussing and analyzing the dialogic efforts between your school and the families you serve.

Dialogue Inside School	Dialogue Outside School	Dialogue Between School and Home
What opportunities are set up for talking with families inside school?	What opportunities are set up for talking with families outside school?	What structures are in place to communicate between home and school for consistent contact?
What is attendance like at such functions?	How are such opportunities received from families' perspectives?	How is such communication received and perceived by families?

Who is positioned as "expert" in such dialogues? In other words, are these functions set up as information-giving where teachers or administrators do the most talking—or are they set up as information-seeking where caretakers and students do the most talking?	Who is positioned as "expert" in such dialogues?	Who is positioned as "expert" in such dialogues?
How are parent-teacher conferences structured? Are they conducive to learning about children's lives, families' hopes for their children, and caretakers' concerns about school?	Are families offered the option of meeting for "conferences" off school property? If not, can you imagine offering such an option? How might doing so be a step in the direction of breaking down the "us" and "them" dichotomy?	How often, why, and when do families initiate communication with school? How can these efforts be analyzed through the three layers of critical literacy and used productively by teachers and administrators? For example, if initiations tend to be focused as reactions to a negative perception of something happening in school (e.g., a teacher isn't being fair to their child), how is power, perspective, and positioning operating and what can we do to change the patterns?

During my work at Bruger Elementary School in St. Francis, I put structures in place that worked for me as a teacher-researcher and worked for many of the caretakers as well. These initiatives were grounded in my commitment to learning from families first, and serving as an information-giver about school policies, achievement, and so on, second. This may at first seem out-of-balance, but given the century or so that school authorities have largely played the role of expert, I consider it a long-overdue shift in power, perspective, and positioning relations:

- *Open-Door Policy in the Classroom*: Caretakers could come in any time they wanted. If they wished to observe or work with students, I asked them to come on in and join the activities. If they wanted to discuss something with me, I politely asked them to wait until I had a free moment. If it was urgent, I asked the children I was working with to work independently until I returned. Regardless of their intention when they came to the door, I *always acknowledged them* with a smile to reinforce the fact that they were welcome in the classroom. This may seem silly and simplistic, but I have sat in numerous classrooms where a caretaker was completely ignored by the teacher until finally, he or she would leave the room. Our actions must reflect our words—that families are welcome in our school and classrooms.

- *Home-School Weekly Journals*: Each Friday I would write a short note to the family in a spiral-bound notebook. The family then had all weekend (or, theoretically, until the following Friday) to write something in the journal. Options for writing were unlimited, including asking me questions, writing about concerns, writing stories together, telling about their weekend activities, or sharing information about the family that I might want to know as the teacher. About half of the families responded every week—others were more sporadic but meaningful when they did respond. Even if there was no response, I asked children to return the journal. Family responses included questions about social issues in the classroom, academics, questions about my own parenting strategies, short passages about their child's growth, long passages about family histories that included tragedy and depression, fictional stories written with child and caretaker, and lists of what the family had done over the weekend. One father who responded only once at the end of the quarter—Alexis' father—wrote about the weekly feeding of their family pet, a snake. This knowledge opened up a whole new communication channel between Alexis, her primary caretaker, and me—something that I could ask them about, learn about, and use as a sort of icebreaker for other conversations.

- *Parent-Teacher Conference Choices*: On the letter I sent home for the traditional parent-teacher conferences, I offered nontraditional options, including the *place* of the conference and whether or not the child would be present. As for the physical setting for the conference, I offered the classroom, their home, or a place of their choosing in the community. Though most opted for the school, a small number asked for home conferences, including one parent who had never attended a school function as long as her children had attended Bruger Elementary (nearly six years at the time of this study). One caretaker asked to meet at a local diner. Some asked for children to be present (usually because of childcare issues) and others wanted to talk alone. But everyone had options.

● *Home Visits*: Before the school year began I drove to see every child's home for myself given the address in their files. This offered me the opportunity to get to know the streets and locales of the community as well as to have a visual image of the place where each child spent the majority of her time. I later conducted official and unofficial home visits. Official visits were limited to the girls who were the focus of this research study and families who simply invited me—these visits were usually framed by an informal "interview" that I had planned. Unofficial home visits occurred as I took monthly or bi-weekly walks and drives around the neighborhood following a school day's end. I would stop and talk with anyone willing, and would purposely travel near the homes of my students.

● *Community Meetings*: Community Council meetings were held monthly and I tried to attend as many as possible. Had I been working with a group of colleagues or in a school where breaking down the Us-Them barriers was an important priority, I could have imagined small groups attending the meetings and sharing the monthly commitment. Mostly I listened at these meetings and engaged in small talk with community members while I learned a great deal about community politics and history. Once I was asked to present to the attendees the work I had been doing with the girls; the community photographs and the girls' writings intrigued everyone.

● *Positive Phone Calls and Notes*: Given sporadic telephone service or the frequent changing of telephone numbers, phone calls were not reliable. However, I always tried. Once a week I would make a few calls or send notes to those I couldn't reach so that each family would have a "positive" contact each month. Many parents complained that they only received negative communication from school, focused on misbehavior, missing homework, demands for school fees, and so on. Committing to consistent, positive communication from school to home was one of the most important things I did to break down the barriers between families and myself. I was no longer perceived as the enemy—the one calling with bad news, the one punishing their child, the one demanding more of their time. I had located positive attributes in their child and genuinely *liked* him or her. I was a real person with real feelings. I knew concrete details about their child's life. I was empathetic. And when I did ask families to help with behavior issues in the classroom, I experienced much less resistance. We were, it seemed, becoming a team.

Each of these structures was set in place to accomplish three major goals:

- To learn about the child's life outside of school so I did not rely on stereotypes of the families; this would serve my curriculum-building as well as relationship-building.

- To attempt to make myself more *concrete* to the families so they did not have to rely on stereotypes of teachers and school authorities.

- To break down the barriers that have traditionally existed between working-class and poor communities and the schools that serve them.

Resisting Stereotypes: Engaging in Everyday Critical Literacy

As a society, we are bombarded by images, stories, and stereotypes of working-class and poor men, women, and children. We must band together and refuse these mainstream definitions of lives often lived through struggle. Having a critical literacy stance will help us take nothing for granted and focus on learning details for ourselves and not relying on the stereotypes created by others.

This book is one example of a critical literacy practice. The text is an attempt to *deconstruct* mainstream stereotypes about life in a poor community, to deconstruct assumptions about urban families who are assumed to not "care." Not only have I attempted to deconstruct mainstream beliefs, but I have written a counter-narrative, a *reconstruction* of living class on the margins and the impact of such on people's physical, psychological, and social lives. And by offering educators food for thought and making concrete suggestions for working with children and families, I am working toward *social action* and change in our educational system. These three tenets are always informed by the layers of critical literacy—sometimes these are embedded in texts that have little meaning in our lives, and other times, like the examples in this chapter, these are real people negotiating life and the three layers, perspective, positioning, and power offer the tools to reconsider our relations with others in the name of education and social justice.

Chapter 10 will move between real lives and textual practices in the classroom as I focus on deconstruction in the Reading Workshop.

10 | Critical Literacy in the Reading Workshop
Deconstructing/Reconstructing Henry and Mudge

One version of Lori's philosophy of education was presented in Chapter 6, which focused on gaining students' interest by starting with their lives. The following quote extends her thinking but it turns our attention to the "perfect lives" of book characters that Lori believed many children encountered each day in their language arts education:

> Because [kids in St. Francis] see things all the time—and they read these little stories in school about all these perfect lives, and mommy and daddy work and blah—*that* is not how it *is*. You have a mom who gets a check once a month whose daddy's on the street corner selling *drugs* whose kid is—you know—sittin' there with people comin' in and out of the house who *buy* drugs and they see this, yet they're goin' to school learnin' about perfect little Jill's life and this and that—and that's *bull*crap because that's not how it is.

Lori chose a hypothetical "Jill" to represent all that is disconnected from the lives of children in St. Francis within the books they often read in classrooms, and she intuitively understood that constant interaction with these mainstream stories was not healthy for children who lived very different lives. In an ironic twist, Lori's daughter Cadence was the reader who I first noticed making up "fictions" about her life to seem more like a character that was living a seemingly perfect life—Henry was his name. Like Lori's reference to a "Jill," "Henry" will be used in this chapter, but the Henry I refer to is the main character in a series of books written for early readers that Herbert Kohl would describe as "middle class in character, [that ties] well-being to money and portray[s] lives full of comfort and joy" (Kohl 1996, 25).

The Henry I refer to here is the beloved preadolescent White, middle-class boy from the *Henry and Mudge* series written by Cynthia Rylant.

This chapter will begin by reconsidering the "basics" of reading instruction to include a critical perspective in the reading workshop and exploring what I call the Multicultural Trap of critical literacy. Then I will describe a series of events in the second grade classroom around *Henry and Mudge* and my attempt to add one simple tool for challenging the books' representations of a normal life. And finally, this chapter will end with work that I did with the girls as they were entering fifth grade when we critically analyzed *Henry and Mudge* through "Disconnections" between their lives and the books. These disconnections led to insightful conversations around assumptions and stereotypes based on social class.

■ Back to the Basics of Reading: The Four Resources Model

Allan Luke and Peter Freebody (1990, 1996, 1999) have long advocated for the basics of reading instruction to include four families of practices where students' repertoires of reading skills and strategies are honed. Their work has been highly influential in Australia through policy and curriculum, making a coherent model that includes critical analysis as a basic practice in the teaching and learning of reading. The four families of practices known together as the "Four Resources Model" are not considered to be linear or hierarchical but rather integrated and necessary for readers to engage with text in meaningful ways as *code breakers, text participants, text users,* and *text analysts*. These four "roles" students will be expected to practice means that readers should be equipped to decode text, make meaning from text, use text appropriately and flexibly across contexts, and evaluate text regarding issues of social, cultural, and political power. These four families of practices are meant to serve as references to what is necessary, but not necessarily sufficient, in the development of critical literacy practices in local contexts. The model is founded on the tenets that since all texts are constructed with none being neutral, readers need a repertoire of tools and practices that will help them decode texts *and* navigate the complex terrain of multiple perspectives and power relations central to critical literacy (Bigelow 2005; Comber 1998; Comber and Thompson 2002; O'Brien 2001; Wallowitz 2004).

Reading and agreeing with the suggestion that all four families of practices are basic necessities for developing readers is one thing; figuring out how to make that work with real children in a progressive reading space is something altogether different. After a brief discussion around a critical literacy perspective in the reading workshop, I will share one experience of great tension between supporting early readers with texts they could read with some fluency, while wanting them to develop skills and strategies for questioning and challenging texts that excluded life as they knew it. To put it another way, I wanted readers to be able to read print and to feel comfortable acknowledging and challenging the "perfect lives" represented in the books they were reading, but it didn't always turn out the way I had hoped—mainly due to my falling victim to the multicultural trap that critical literacy can lure us in to.

◼ Weaving the Critical Throughout the Reading Workshop

Reading, and reading a lot is the most important thing students can do as they continuously develop as code breakers, text participants, text users, and text analysts. Reading workshop, as defined by progressive educators in the United States (e.g., Calkins 2001; Taberski 2000) is a framework for organizing the practices of meaningful reading in classrooms and has been celebrated for growing readers through student choice, individualized instruction, and large blocks of time reserved for self-selected independent reading. A critical literacy perspective encompasses these cornerstone aspects of progressive literacy education, and at least for some researchers, stands firmly upon these ideals, as Pam Green writes:

> before critical literacy can occur within the classroom, students need the opportunity to engage in meaningful use of literacy, or in other words, to use literacy in ways that relate to their interests and needs. Without the opportunity to write and read for a range of purposes, with access to a variety of texts, there is no basis upon which critical discussion of and reflection on literacy can occur. (2001, 12)

Many progressive literacy educators already have systems in place (such as Reading Workshop) that can easily incorporate critical literacy—but progressive beliefs and structures are not enough (Finn 1999; Schneider 2001). In a great number of classrooms in the United States, children are reading massive quantities of text, making sense of those texts, and responding in interesting and creative ways to their reading. But in most classrooms students are *not* learning to be text analysts; they are not questioning power relations in the text, stereotypes that are reproduced through text, the multiple ways in which a text could have been construct-ed, and the ways in which a text positions different readers. In many pro-gressive classroom spaces, three of the four families of practices in the Four Resources Model are being engaged—but the fourth, the critical, is too often left out of the literacy teaching and learning happening in our schools.

A critical literacy stance that includes the serious consideration of per-spective, power, and positioning is simply not a part of most students' experiences in school. A secondary problem however, is that oftentimes when a critical perspective *is* a part of reading instruction in the elemen-tary grades, the texts used as exemplars for recognizing marginalized per-spectives are those that would be considered "multicultural" in nature (e.g., Leland, Harste, and Huber 2005; Lewis 2000). These books are often written from the perspective of a character who is not White, and/or who does not experience life in stereotypical, mainstream ways (such as the nuclear family living in a home they own with access to social and eco-nomic resources that protect them from the hardships often faced by working-class and poor families).

I fell victim to this multicultural trap as a second-grade teacher; my stu-dents were exposed to literature with characters and situations that did not reflect mainstream America. We discussed perspectives, critically consid-ered social issues, asked ourselves about the use of power, and explored how the books made us feel and what they made us think. Our critical lit-eracy "work" with written text was often focused around progressive, sophisticated children's literature that was read aloud by me given the challenging text and the students' emerging practices as code breakers. However, I never deconstructed a mainstream text in front of the students, and I never gave them the tools they needed to do it themselves as they read independently in Reading Workshop. When they were faced with books that seemed to present "normal" lives in a mainstream way, the growing readers in the classroom worked hard as code breakers, text par-ticipants, and text users. But they were certainly not text analysts. One example was in their reading of *Henry and Mudge*.

▪ Thinking Critically About *Henry and Mudge*

Henry and Mudge stories are written as readable text, the illustrations support problem solving of difficult words, the main character is a young child, and there are many books within the series. Such characteristics are considered important for early readers as they negotiate sign-symbol relationships and construct understandings of texts, or, to use Luke and Freebody's model, perform as code breakers and text participants. But, like all texts, the *Henry and Mudge* series signifies much more. In this case the storylines are situated within a White family's life that includes a mother, father, young boy, and a dog. The family lives in a free-standing house with a wide front porch, a living room, breakfast nook, dining room, and a bedroom for Henry where he has a twin-size bed and a fish aquarium, a large front yard, and a spacious backyard that is home to a swing dangling from a tree branch and a picnic table, all framed by a white-picket fence. The family eats at the dining room table together, has a separate table and chairs in the kitchen, a full basement for storage, a tool shed with rows of tools, etc. The parents throw elaborate birthday parties for Henry, and have relatives who live in nice homes in the country with materially rich interiors.

In the book *Henry and Mudge and the Best Day of All* (Rylant 1995) Henry invites friends to his home for a birthday party. Guests are welcomed by colorful streamers wrapped around columns on the front porch and balloons stretching into the air from either side of the front steps. The children's creatively decorated packages tied with perfect bows are piled in the living room and they make their way to the backyard for the games set up by Henry's mom and dad.

Though much critical literacy work had been accomplished through whole-class read-alouds, and small and large group discussions as presented in Chapters 2, 4, 8, and 9, students were not reading *Henry and Mudge* books critically, nor had I taught them to do so. Instead, they were constructing fictions of their own lives incorporating themes from the series in an attempt to make "connections" with the books. After reading about Henry's elaborate birthday party with games, prizes, balloons, and many friends leaving the party with goldfish in plastic bags, Cadence told three nearby classmates, "I had goldfish at my party too." The children in the classroom seemed to try desperately to *connect* with Henry and his experiences rather than question them as "normal" or consider them as valuable within themselves but not the definition of a happy child's existence. The day after Cadence's statement about her birthday party, I planned small-group work to suggest two practices they could use to critically read mainstream texts:

1. Permission to question the text and compare it to their own lives, and
2. A simple tool for reconstructing, or changing, the text to align more with students' experiences.

The following transcript is from one of the videotaped small group meetings around *Henry and Mudge* books. Beginning with general questions about the books within the series, I eventually moved toward scaffolding students' critical reading of the text by asking, "What would you change about this story to make it more like your life?" Once I began questioning the text, its representation of "family," and asking the students what they might change, the discussion moved toward text analysis and the critical reading of oneself into a story.

STEPHANIE: So you have told me all the things you like about these stories, what if you could change something about them—what would you change?

SARAH: Like the names of the characters and the characters.

STEPHANIE: Who would you change?

SARAH: The dog or the father.

ANNIE: First change the father.

STEPHANIE: Okay, change the father or the dog. Into—what do you mean?

SARAH: Change him into a scientist (giggles from all three girls).

STEPHANIE: Okay, he could be a scientist. Or maybe he wouldn't have to be there at all, right? You could take the father out of the book altogether?

I inserted this possibility because Sarah's father was in jail at the time and she seemed under pressure to suggest an alternative "father" that would fit within the mainstream discourse of the *Henry and Mudge* series (a white-collar professional father) rather than suggest something that might reflect her world.

SARAH: And add the father as a big brother or somethin'.

Sarah had several older male cousins and uncles that were important in her life, but no older brothers. However, she suggested an alternative to the family structure in the text that she understood intimately.

STEPHANIE: Ohhh. So maybe there could be a big brother instead of a father? I'm wondering if you started writing a new series like this, hmmm. I'm wondering where you could say the father went. Why wasn't the father there?

SARAH: We could say he's at work.

ALEXIS: Or he's lazy.

Sarah and Alexis were speaking within competing discourses around fathers, or men in general, in the community of St. Francis. Sarah suggesting that fathers do, in fact, work, and Alexis suggesting that if they don't work, they are lazy. A more critical reading of not working, however, would recognize the lack of work available to many of the adult men in St. Francis who had not completed high school and relied heavily upon their manual labor and market demands for such things as painting, drywall installation, and so on.

STEPHANIE: Okay, he could be lazy or he could be at work.

ANNIE:　　 Or he could be in jail.

STEPHANIE: He could be in jail.

SARAH:　　 He could be in a car.

STEPHANIE: Okay, so if you each started thinking about . . . hmmm. I love to read *Henry and Mudge* stories too, I think they're great stories—but, when I look at this family it doesn't really look like my family. I don't know if it looks like Alexis' family.

Following this prompt, the girls' enthusiasm increased as well as their use of gestures and they began moving around on the floor. Considering a change in one character was fine, specific. But opening up the possibility that the entire family structure can be called into question seemed to excite them.

ALEXIS:　　 No. I have *mass* more people.

STEPHANIE: How 'bout you Annie? Does this look like your family?

ANNIE:　　 No (shakes head no and opens eyes wide).

STEPHANIE: How 'bout you, Sarah?

SARAH:　　 No.

STEPHANIE: So maybe Cynthia Rylant wrote about a family she knew, but if we started to write stories like this we'd have to change it a lot, wouldn't we? To write about things that we really know.

SARAH:　　 It looks like my aunt's 'cuz they live in a house and um, they gots a backyard with a dog in it and stuff.

STEPHANIE: Really? So this looks like your aunt's family?

SARAH:　　 Yeah, my aunt _____, she lives in Florida.

Sarah had discussed her aunt before, noting that she lives in a neighborhood with "big houses" and near "doctors and lawyers."

STEPHANIE: So is there anything else you might change in these stories?

ANNIE:　　 Switch these [picture on cover of book].

STEPHANIE: What?

ANNIE: [points to Henry and his female cousin]

STEPHANIE: Oh. Have the *girl* in the real story, in the main story? Oh, Annie, I see what you mean. Here's Henry in the center of the picture, it's all about Henry. And the girl cousin is in the background. So you would switch those?

ANNIE: Yeah.

STEPHANIE: So your main character would be a girl?

ANNIE: Yeah.

STEPHANIE: Oh, that would change things, huh? Great idea.

As a teacher, I was encouraged by Annie's suggestion that gender made a difference in this story and that she would like to see the main character represented as a girl. This was reflective of the work we had done together as a class and in small groups around gender discrimination and the value of gender-specific experiences. At this point in the conversation I wanted the girls to move into independent reading, and I hoped, but didn't necessarily expect, that the work we had done together around questioning, challenging, and changing the text in small ways would be taken up during quiet reading time. I was pleasantly surprised, however, that Sarah in particular took on the role of facilitator (or "teacher") during a small group collaborative reading. With her willingness to mimic my questions and prompts, Sarah continued to plant the seeds of critical literacy that I had started in the discussion about the *Henry and Mudge* books.

■ Reading and Discussing *Henry and Mudge* Independently

Minutes following our small group meeting, Annie, Sarah, Alexis, Tina, and Brian began reading while sitting in a circle on the floor. They chose to read *Henry and Mudge and the Best Day of All* and began reading round-robin style—likely based on their early socialization in first grade to take turns around a circle when reading. The following transcript is from an audiotape recording of their discussion after they read the entire book. Sarah attempts to scaffold the group to consider "changes" to the story—something I hadn't requested that they do, but she has taken it upon herself to continue the theme from our small group meeting.

SARAH: Alright, we gotta talk about it alright? Now Annie, we're gonna

	make you talk some alright? Alright. Annie. Talk. Like, what could we change if we made up the story?
TINA:	We . . .
SARAH:	Annie.
ANNIE:	Change . . . (inaudible) to the front cover (she's talking about the girl and boy in the illustration).
SARAH:	Like what *word* can we change?

Sarah continued to position herself in the role of a teacher or facilitator, but had no success in getting the other students to "change" something that was meaningful (in Sarah's eyes) in the story. She didn't give up, however, and prodded the students to deepen their thinking and finally ended with her own suggestion for a change in the story:

SARAH:	Now wait, what could we—what else could we change? I know there are more things, cuz we had a talk about this this morning, didn't we Annie?
TINA:	You gotta change somethin'.
SARAH:	I *will* change somethin'.
SARAH:	That Henry didn't *have* goldfish [at his birthday party]— that Henry *went*—
BRIAN:	[inaudible—anticipating Sarah's suggestion of fishing]
SARAH:	That's why I wanted to make a connection, that's what I wanted to say. Tina, you know what I wanted to change? I wanted to change that Henry *didn't* have goldfish—he went *fish*in'. That's what I wanted to change.

Though Sarah's change may seem inconsequential to someone not familiar with cultural practices in St. Francis, the change she suggested was closely in line with her experiences of family gatherings, special occasions, and celebrations: going fishing. Sarah challenged the assumption in the book that happy birthdays are spent in someone's backyard with costly games, prizes, and gifts, and replaced that privileged practice with her family's preference for spending time together fishing. With the exception of Annie, who was also in our small group earlier on this same day, Sarah didn't succeed in getting others to suggest changes that might call into question the authority of Rylant's text. However, it is promising to know that both Sarah and Annie quickly used the tools of our small group to challenge, and change, *Henry and Mudge*, a series of texts that had, up to this point, been considered innocent, neutral, and the construction of normalcy.

Rereading *Henry and Mudge* as Almost-Fifth-Graders: The Critical Disconnect

On a hot, sticky July morning in the summer before the girls entered fifth grade, I met Heather, Sarah, Alexis, and Cadence at a park across the street from Bruger Elementary School. Each of the girls was wearing very short jean shorts and a short-sleeved t-shirt, and as they walked toward our meeting place I noticed a distinct difference in their gait and overall presence from our previous meeting six months before when the girls were in the middle of their fourth grade year. A sophisticated and carefree aura surrounded each of them, but particularly Heather and Sarah, who began talking right away about their summer social lives playing volleyball, rollerskating, going to the local amusement park, and giggling about boys on whom they had "crushes." These girls had obviously done a lot of "growing up" in the previous months, and I began to wonder whether or not they would even be interested in doing the reflective, critical work I was hoping for on this particular day. Armed with a rolling suitcase filled with books of all kinds, including *Henry and Mudge* books, I sat cross-legged on the shaded concrete, my head flying side-to-side following the conversations that bounced from one girl to the next. Why would they even be remotely interested in thinking back to the life of dear Henry that they had read and talked about so long ago? On that morning I learned a very important lesson, however, and that was that when critical literacy engagements are embedded in students' lives and driven by their observations and comments, that students (even almost-fifth-grade girls) will find such work interesting, motivating, and deeply stimulating.

After about twenty minutes of catching up in high-speed, multilayered, loud conversations, Cadence offered me an entry point into the work I had hoped we would do together on this particular day. Talking about her fifth or sixth birthday party and getting hit in the head with the swinging stick meant to crack open a dangling piñata, Cadence gave me the opportunity to open a conversation around the *Henry and Mudge* books, "Oh, that reminds me of something I wanted to ask you about today . . . " I insert quickly so as to not miss the opportunity. Quickly unzipping the suitcase and pulling out a dozen or so books about Henry and his dog Mudge, I asked the girls if they remembered reading the series when they were in second grade.

"Oh, we *loved* those books!" squealed Heather.

"I read *that* one!" said Cadence snatching up one of the books.

"I read that, and that, and that . . . ," said Sarah.

Digging through the pile of books was fun for the girls, they talked about different storylines, characters, and memories of loving these books when they were "little." After a brief trip down memory lane, I described the book I was writing for teachers (the one you are reading now) and how I had been thinking about readers making connections during their reading. The girls quickly barked out different "connections" they make as readers: "life connections between you and the book" or text-to-self connections; "texts to other books" or text-to-text connections, and book-to-world connections. They were eager to offer examples, but I wanted to go back, again, to something I had witnessed in second grade. I told them the story about Cadence telling her reading partner that she had "goldfish at her party too" just like Henry at his birthday party in *The Best Day of All*. Cadence giggled knowingly as I told the story, and I continued:

> and I thought, hmmm. I wonder if that is really a connection to the book or is Cadence feeling like she has to make up something in her life to *fit* the book? So then I started listening to other people's conversations and sometimes it seemed to me that people would make up things to make a connection to the book. So then I thought, 'Wait a second, maybe I should be teaching kids to find the disconnection.' So you can find the connections with your life, but you can also find the disconnect. The part that doesn't go with your life. And you can talk about that—how it's not the same as your life, and how, um, that can help your understanding. What do you think about that? Have you ever thought about disconnections?

The girls were listening intently but admittedly had never really considered how books did *not* connect with their life experiences. I asked them to give it a try as they flipped through the pages of *Henry and Mudge* books looking at the illustrations. The first disconnection verbalized was by Sarah, when she was referring to an illustration in *Henry and Mudge Get the Cold Shivers* where Henry's mother delivered several kinds of food and drink to a sick Henry in bed: "My mom don't bring me all that stuff to my room—she won't bring me no popsicle, no crackers, actually, she'll just— I don't even *know*." The girls were adept at articulating connections with the book, but faced with the task of describing the disconnect between the text and one's life; Sarah struggled with finding the words for articulating such difference. "I don't even know" is indicative of that struggle—how can you describe difference in a meaningful way?

Shortly afterward, Cadence commented on an illustration of Henry, his mother, father, uncle, and cousin eating at a dining room table: "I have a disconnection. Uh, my family, they just don't always *eat* at one big table. We always go in the living room."

"Let's talk about that," I suggested, turning the book around so that Heather and Sarah could also see the illustration. They immediately jumped in with their own disconnections, "Yeahhh!" agreed Heather, and Sarah added, "Oh yeah, we eat and watch TV." The girls had a ball talking about all the different places they and their families regularly eat meals and reasons why: small spaces with only a couple chairs and mail piled high on the table were common experiences. One that I hadn't heard of in St. Francis but forced me to go way back in my own life was Cadence's story about eating with her sisters on the roof outside the second floor window. I had nearly forgotten about all the snacks and meals and playtime I had with my older cousins after we would crawl through their third floor window and perch ourselves on the gray-shingled, burning-hot, nearly flat surface. Toward the end of this part of the discussion, Heather reminded us all that there is never one "truth" however, and that for her family at least, they "sometimes eat like that at Thanksgiving or something."

The girls, anxious to articulate disconnections now, tapped into an important insight about illustrations and how they can be read as "text"—illustrations do not only reflect the materiality of lives and hint at social-classed living, but they also frame family *practices*. These cultural ways of being, not simply the one-dimensional simplistic illustration itself that includes people and objects, were invoked from the image and became the topic of conversation with the girls as they considered connections and disconnections between their family practices and those represented in the images of the text. Soon the group moved into a critical conversation dealing with social class stereotypes as they recognized Henry's cousin, who seemed different from everyone else in Henry's family.

Class Stereotypes: Assumptions, Challenges, and a Frilly-Dressed Little Rich Girl

Studying the same illustration of Henry, his mother, father, uncle, and cousin sitting at a long dining room table, Cadence piqued the group's interest in the girl cousin who was wearing a bow in her curly hair and a frilly white dress.

"She's like different. She acts like she's different from the rest of the family," Cadence pointed out.

"She don't eat all that stuff," suggested Heather.

"What do you mean?" I asked.

"She eats like lobster," Heather told us.

"Oh, you think she eats lobster?" I asked.

"Yeah, she looks like a little rich girl," Heather sneered.

"Oh, she looks like a little rich girl, what do you mean by that?" I probed.

Heather responded by describing her white frilly dress, her hair bow, and Cadence joined in. Sarah, however, sat quietly.

"Do you think she looks like a rich girl?" I asked Sarah. She responded by shaking her head no quietly. "Tell us about that."

"'Cuz, I ain't rich, but I ain't poor, but I got dresses," she tells us matter-of-factly.

"She looks like a little spoiled brat. Look at her purse," added Heather, "this is how she walks, I'm serious," she told us as she stood up to perform what she considered a spoiled brat walk. Again, Heather is reading the illustration to understand not only material lives, but also the social practices of the characters.

"I never look like *that* until like Easter or Christmas," Cadence told the group.

"She just looks like she's not used to—she looks like she's from a fancier place," stated Sarah.

"To eat lobster!" yelled Heather, glad that Sarah is finally seeing her point.

"And eat out," added Cadence.

The girls continued to look through the books when Heather found the evidence she had hoped for, "Oh my God! She *is* spoiled, that's her *room!* Look at her teacups and her hankies."

"Do you have a disconnect, Heather?" I asked her.

"Yeah, I ain't got all that stuff on my wall."

Sarah jumped in, "Heather, but you're spoiled too."

"No I'm not!"

"Yes you are!"

"There's her bed. She is spoiled," Heather pointed to a canopy bed in the cousin's spacious bedroom.

"I have a canopy too, but mine ain't just like that. But I got the circle," Sarah told us.

The conversation continued and began to incorporate money when Cadence stated that she was not like that girl (in the book) at all, because she didn't get everything she wanted and she had to do chores around the

house to even get any money from her mom. The other girls had a different experience with money, however, and Sarah told us that she was given
$40.00 each week by her father to have fun with and pay her cellular
phone bill. This was a great opportunity for me to challenge the girls,
again, to consider multiple perspectives and to resist stereotyping or essentializing people the way that they had been essentialized by people for so
long.

"You have a *phone*?" I asked, surprised.

"I do too," said Heather.

"I been having a phone since I was eight," Sarah added.

"Now some people, Sarah, might say that only really rich kids have
phones," I stated.

"Nu-huh," said Heather.

"Oh, that is *not* true!" Sarah shouted in disbelief.

"Why?" I asked.

"'Cuz," Sarah shrugged.

"We're not really rich and we both have a phone," Heather told me.

"My cousin, her mom used to be real bad on drugs and then she got
better, she's been better for a couple months, and they got 'em an apartment and stuff, and she ain't got a job yet, but my cousin gots a phone,
and her brother gots a PlayStation 2 and stuff like that, and they ain't
rich," Sarah told the group.

I pulled out a notebook and pen, "So there are lots of in-betweens. So
if you have rich over here (I draw a line on a piece of notebook paper)—
and you have really poor over here (another line is drawn on the opposite
side of the paper). There's lots of stuff in the middle, right?"

"And you're doing okay, like," added Heather.

"Like not so rich and not so poor," Cadence finished.

After this acknowledgement of the gray areas between the extremes of
rich and poor, the girls began talking about people who "act" rich, or
"goody-goody" even when they are not. The conversation shifts from
material possessions and money to the *performance* of social class—something that makes thinking about such issues even more complex.

I began to probe them about the goody-goody concept, "And you said
'"goody-goody."' Does that mean that you have to be rich to act goody-
goody?"

"No," Sarah stated slowly with her eyebrows raised.

"Confusing isn't it?" I asked the girls.

"Like goody-goody, is like when you're not really rich, but you're really perfect and you just act like you're rich and act like you got everything but you don't," Sarah explained.

"Like, you said this cousin [in the *Henry and Mudge* book] looks goody-goody," I said.

"Yeah," said Sarah.

"Because if somebody is like . . . " Cadence began.

"She has *teacups* on her wall!" shouted Heather.

"What does that mean though?" I asked.

"She's rich!" Heather yelled.

"She could be spoiled, but her family could, probably couldn't be rich, they probably just like her to," Sarah began.

"Do stuff," Heather added, again focusing on the performance of social class.

"People don't have to be rich and there's uhhh, ugh!" Cadence was starting to get quite frustrated. It had all seemed so simple before this discussion.

I laughed a little and Heather mimics what she perceived as a performance of a rich girl, "People be like," she continued in a high-pitched sing-songy voice, batting her eyelashes and exaggerating the pronunciation of each word, "'Mommy, can I have the money to get a dress?' Just like on the Fresh Prince of Bel Air," Heather brought in her knowledge of girl performances in a wealthy household from a television show.

Throughout this conversation that began with a frilly-dressed girl in a simple illustration, the girls began to articulate their local understandings of social class difference and the roles that material goods, money, and performance play in social class. Beginning with assumptions and stereotypes, the girls were able to work through when and why some were simply wrong and that a perspective that takes into account individual people and practices and relativity might be more productive than the rich-poor dichotomy and how people are perceived and judged based on where they might be considered within the spectrum.

Should We Burn *Henry and Mudge*?[1]

Lori's quote framed this chapter, focusing on the perfect lives often portrayed in children's literature and the disconnection between such portrayals and the experiences of most children in St. Francis. As a progressive, critically focused teacher, I agreed with Lori's insight and worked hard to fill the classroom library with books that reflected many ways of living lives, and used those texts as the focal point during my read-alouds and minilessons across the curriculum and the school day. My eye was always on *other* ways of representing experiences, and I feel confident that the children learned a great deal and grew from such engagements. However, what I failed to attend to at the time was the fact that most texts the children will encounter inside and outside school are mainstream in nature and privilege a hypothetical "hegemonic" American way of living. And though Lori was on the right track with her critique of the stories about "Jill's" perfect life in school books, the bigger picture is even more daunting: television commercials, newspaper advertisements, sitcoms, cartoons, movies, billboards, magazines, song lyrics, music videos, and so forth are the texts of their worlds that are often placing idealized versions of a White middle-class life as standard or normal, to which people will compare their own daily existences.

Burning *Henry and Mudge* because of children's unarticulated comparisons of their own lives to Henry's is not viable. In fact, neither is choosing not to use the books in a classroom. The fact of the matter is that readers of all ages need to understand how power, perspective, and positioning operate in all texts—but most definitely in texts that promote unitary versions of successful lives and those that perpetuate stereotypes of any kind. *Henry and Mudge* can continue to serve important purposes for developing readers as code breakers, text participants, and text users, but it can also be used for developing text analysts—a crucial aspect of basic literacy practice.

■ Moving Forward with the Basics: Critical Literacy, the Multicultural Trap, and Disconnections

The basics of literacy instruction, and reading instruction in this chapter, must include a critical perspective that offers students the tools to deconstruct and reconstruct texts and work toward socially just understandings. In second grade, the first tools I offered students included acknowledging difference and reconstructing (or "changing") the text in some way that aligned more with the reader's life. In the summer following their fourth grade year, the girls and I worked together to deconstruct mainstream illustrations and stereotypes and reconstruct the concept of what is "normal" (this was not included here). Instead of generations of children continuing to be raised by and compare their lives with images and books representing perfect lives, readers need basic repertoires of practices to ask critical questions of texts, creators of texts, and of themselves as readers of texts.

Critical literacy practices in the United States have often been focused around the use of multicultural literature and there are many reasons why such literature is imperative in any classroom. However, never using mainstream texts for critical literacy purposes created a serious problem in my second-grade classroom as students were not working to challenge such texts but were instead comparing their own lives to the characters' lives in the books. Multicultural literature has a lure of its own, but especially in the critically focused reading and writing classroom, this rich body of literature can offer much to readers and writers. However, there is a potential Multicultural Trap lingering in the wings of such practices, and that is the trap of forgetting to help students critique and challenge mainstream texts—those texts they will encounter most often throughout their lives.

Disconnection from such texts can open up spaces for critical conversations around books, images, and social practices. The connection-making pedagogy that has pervaded reading instruction must begin to include disconnection, the articulation of disconnection, and the important conversations that can take place around such acknowledgements. We are often hyperaware of our difference from others, whether in text or life, but these differences are also difficult to understand and even more challenging to discuss. Talking across difference, however, can lead us to insights, just as the girls in this chapter began to realize that "rich" and "poor" stereotypes were not necessarily a productive way of thinking about different people, including themselves. And that conversation began with a comment about a disconnection between a reader and a frilly-dressed girl sitting at a dining room table.

Exercise 10.1 Deconstructing Children's Literature

Miss Nelson Is Missing! (Allard 1985) was a favorite book of a graduate student in one of my classes. Each fall she would read this book to her second grade students, laughing along with them at the images of the "substitute" teacher as she was portrayed throughout the text. Given an assignment to critically read a text, this student purposefully chose a beloved book because she did not believe there was anything about it necessary for critique. In the end, however, she was appalled at how the two different "teachers" were presented and recognized the use of standard images of female beauty in the illustrations. Though surprised at what she had not noticed before about gendered stereotypes, this teacher decided not to avoid the book but rather to engage her students in a critical reading of the text. All texts are constructed, and they all use perspective and power to position readers and characters inside the text in particular ways.

Choose a book that you often use in your classroom. Work through a deconstruction of the book's images and words by using questions from Chapter 7 about perspective, power, and positioning. Then consider the following:

1. Why were you drawn to this book in the first place?
2. Were you surprised by your deconstruction?
3. What roles did connection-making and disconnection-making play in your choosing of this book and then of your deconstruction of this book?
4. How have you used the book in the past?
5. How might you use the book in the future to incorporate the development of critical literacy and readers as text analysts?

It would be helpful to share critical insights of various books with colleagues and to work with others to deconstruct mainstream world texts such as television commercials, popular cartoons (I recently worked with a group of teachers to deconstruct *Dora the Explorer*), newspaper advertisements, and films. Like the enthusiasm and joy the girls demonstrated in their critical re-readings of *Henry and Mudge*, you may find critically reading texts of all kinds to be stimulating, challenging, and even enjoyable.

This chapter has foregrounded two tenets of critical literacy, deconstruction and reconstruction, and has provided evidence for the necessity of rethinking the basics of reading instruction while cautioning educators of at least one potential trap. Reconstruction and social action will be the focus of Chapter 11 as we reconsider writing workshop and the role of critical literacy within a progressive writing classroom.

▤ Note

1 Borrowed from Herbert Kohl's title, *Should We Burn Babar? Essays on Children's Literature and the Power of Stories* (1996).

11

Critical Literacy in the Writing Workshop
Reconstruction and Social Action

I had been a child who believed in books, but I had never really found me or mine in print. My family was always made over into caricatures or flattened into saintlike stock creatures. I never found my lovers in their strength and passion. Outside my mother's stubbornness and my own outraged arrogance, I had never found any reason to believe in myself. But I had the idea that I could make it exist on those pages.

—Dorothy Allison (1988)

The children's pictures and words were hardly adequate to convey the difficulty of their situation, but their photo-essays were a starting point for acknowledging and discussing, in their own voices, a very tough predicament.

—Wendy Ewald and Alexandra Lightfoot (2001, 12)

It was a sweltering June day in the ground-floor classroom at Bruger Elementary. Two fans were humming, moving hair and papers at 30-second intervals. A clothesline stretched from the far wall to the open windows where mounted photographs clipped by clothespins hung side by side—a primitive art gallery featuring the community of St. Francis. Callie was hunched over her writer's notebook staring intently at a photograph of her older sister and her sister's tall, blonde-haired, blue-eyed boyfriend. Rose lounged on a football-shaped beanbag drafting a book review of a book from the *Powerpuff Girls* series. Joanie and Alexis whispered quietly, marking on their pieces of writing with colored pencils as they worked through a final editing. Cadence twirled in a rolling chair as Faith read over Cadence's story about a fire at her house. I sat quietly watching the scene of engagement—a rare moment when every single girl was moving toward her self-imposed goals for our publication of a literary magazine. A smile of disbelief crept over my face and I shook my head slowly from side to side.

"What?" Cadence stopped twirling and stared at me—sun-bleached hair sticking out on all sides. "What!?" She repeated louder, opening her eyes wide and cocking her head.

"Nothin'," I said. "I'm just proud of you."

Cadence smiled and started her twirling again and I noticed a little smirk peeking out from Rose's face, and Callie turned and looked at us with a closed-mouth smile.

Maybe they were proud of themselves.

Maybe they were proud of me.

Maybe they realized that I hadn't given up on them—that I *knew* they had the power to engage themselves in a pedagogy that centered their lives and encouraged them to reconstruct the world around us. Surely they knew that there had been many times during the two years (at that point) that I had felt like throwing in the towel—even threatened to do it once. At times their resistance (which I prefer to call an agentive act of hijacking) drove me mad, beat me down, wore me out, even made me cry. The voices in my mind would argue with one another all the way home where I would bury myself in the writings of bell hooks, Paulo Freire, Donaldo Macedo, Ira Shor, and Myles Horton. Their words reminded me that resistance to (or complete hijacking of) a critical pedagogy is *normal*; that students often have a difficult time moving from being an *object of* education to being a *subject within* education.

Sitting in that room with beads of sweat dripping from my hairline, it dawned on me that we were all proud of ourselves. And of each other.

Wendy Ewald has worked with many children to construct photographic representations and accompanying essays of their lived experiences, giving them the opportunity to choose how those experiences would be presented to others in a public sense (Ewald 2001). In a way, Ewald is working to prevent children on the margins of mainstream society from experiencing Dorothy Allison's childhood dilemma. This dilemma, faced by Allison and continuously faced by the girls in St. Francis, was that the places, people, and experiences in books did not look—at all—like their realities. By publishing children's photographs and essays (Ewald 2001) and numerous novels and short stories (Allison 1993, 2002), Ewald and Allison challenge and reconstruct the dominance of mainstream lives in public texts. This reconstruction of perceptions around what kinds of lives have the right to be published can also be conceived of as social action, since the publication of such texts moves beyond the private and local into public spaces. Reconstruction and social action that would validate writers' experiences and challenge social hierarchies based in social class, race, and gender were always forefront in my mind as I worked in St. Francis. In the regular classroom and in my work with Heather, Cadence, Rose, Faith, Sarah, Alexis, Joanie, and Callie, my intention was to do three things:

1. *To open up a writing space where any topic was "allowed."* This goal was based on my personal experiences in classrooms where certain topics were discouraged and considered taboo by both teachers and students, and grounded in literacy research around students' and teachers' implicit understandings about "appropriate" topics for the writing workshop (Jones 2003/2004, 2004; Schneider 2001; Skinner 2006).

2. *To use my knowledge of students' lives and power relations inside school to help construct well-composed texts that might challenge the status quo.* This goal emerged within a nexus of literacy research that includes the following: the new literacy studies focused on local knowledge of power relations and literacies (e.g., Barton and Hamilton 1998; Street 2003, 2005), the writing process field that focuses on the writer's expression and craft (e.g., Atwell 1998; Calkins 1994; Graves 1994; Murray 1985), and critically focused work within personal writing that relocates the personal within broader social relations that are always grounded in gender, class, race, sexuality, ability, religion, and other identity markers that are used for positioning people within hierarchical structures of value (e.g., Heffernan 2004; Heffernan and Lewison 2003; Hicks 2001; Jones 2004; Kamler 2001; Lensmire 1994, 2000).

3. *To encourage students to use their texts as forms of social action.* A great deal of literature exists to support this goal as teachers and students have worked together not only to challenge various practices, but also to reconstruct those practices through various projects (e.g., Allen 1999; Comber and Simpson 2001; Powell, Cantrell, and Adams 2001; Vasquez 2004).

This chapter will reconceptualize writing workshop in a way that intertwines personal experience with social relations and critical analysis, then moves back into a classroom in St. Francis where the girls and I engaged in a critically focused writing workshop pedagogy that reflected the three goals. Finally, this chapter will culminate with a social action project, publishing a literary magazine and holding a public open-house for people from the community and the larger surrounding city to interact with a photography "gallery," a collection of the girls' favorite books from the year, a website, and a copy of the literary magazine—all created (with some adult help) by the girls.

◼ Writing Workshop and Student Texts: A Critical Look

Assuming a critical literacy perspective in writing pedagogy takes on various levels of analysis in the classroom. First, the teacher's understanding of power, perspective, and positioning of students in the writing workshop environment is crucial. Researchers have written extensively about the inequities, stereotypes, and discriminatory practices that are too-often reproduced in progressive writing workshop spaces (e.g., Dyson 2001, 2003; Kamler 2001; Lensmire 1994). This body of research has advocated for teachers and students to critically examine the impact of peer relations in the classroom on both writing processes and products. For example, Timothy Lensmire (2000) argues that the writing workshop focus on individual students, their writing, and the teacher's job of "following the lead of the child" ignores the social nature of the workshop environment and the relations within the environment that both empower and constrain individual writers. Lensmire writes about student affiliations within writing workshop and systematic ways through which some students are marginalized and silenced, not encouraged and supported to write from their lives—one goal of writing workshop. He also writes about teacher-student interactions and the inner struggle some students may face if a teacher recommends revising and elaborating a piece that seems (to the teacher) more "powerful" or personal than a piece chosen by the student. The example used by Lensmire is a teacher-student writing conference where the teacher encouraged the writer to choose a notebook entry based on her father as a narrative that could be developed outside the notebook. The teacher did not know, however, that the father was abusive and that the student did not want to write in a public way about her father. Thus, not only do peer relations work to empower some and marginalize others (one example in this book is in Chapter 4), but teacher-student conferences do the same.

Beyond critical analysis of power, perspective, and positioning within the workshop environment, a critically focused writing teacher will also be attending closely to the texts produced by individual students. Stereotypes around race, class, gender, sexuality, religion, and ability are pervasive in our society and are apt to find their way into the written texts composed by students. Just as no published children's literature should be considered innocent or benign (as in Chapter 10), no children's productions of text should be assumed free of damaging content. Unlike a traditional writing workshop assumption that student writing is uniquely a part of the writer, a critical perspective assumes that the writing is always informed by both local and broad social relations. Thus, a traditional writing workshop teacher may be hesitant to question or challenge the content in a student's writing whereas a critically focused writing teacher would attempt to recognize content that perpetuates a discriminatory social hierarchy and to work toward collaborative understanding and reconstruction (see Chapter 7 for possible questions or prompts). If such deconstruction and reconstruction processes are taking place across the school day with various texts including oral language, then writers will also understand their compositions as pieces that can be deconstructed and reconstructed for the work of social justice.

The following sections will highlight student writing samples from the girls in St. Francis that exemplify the three goals stated at the beginning of this chapter for a critically focused writing workshop:

1. Writing about any topic is allowed.
2. Questioning and reconstructing texts that are well composed and carry potential to challenge the status quo is promoted.
3. Using texts for social action beyond the local classroom and private uses is encouraged.

▉ Any Topic Is Allowed: Tulips, a Natural Death, a Murder, and Hating Ms. Jones

The girls' writer's notebooks and published pieces were peppered with content that might make some teachers squirm: Family members in jail, fighting, disgruntled narratives about school, family, friends, and police officers, drugs, alcohol, dead cats in yards, dead birds on sidewalks, and the death of family members. Their writing was also peppered with pieces that might make some teachers widen their eyes and nod their heads in approval: Descriptive pieces about nature, narratives about family gatherings, and memoirs of holiday celebrations. In the interest of time and space, four pieces of writing will be offered here as one spectrum ("most appealing" to "least appealing") representative of content in the girls' writing. This spectrum is based in teachers' and students' unspoken understandings of what topics are most appropriate for writing workshop.

"Tulips," written by Cadence to accompany a photograph she took at a local art museum, was drafted in a writer's notebook and later revised and published. The piece is filled with strong action verbs and descriptive language; the formation of the poem itself is tall and straight on the left margin and waving, or moving on the right margin; and it begins and ends with the same word: tulips. From a writing process perspective, this piece is a great success for a second grade writer. The craft of the composition has been carefully thought through.

Tulips
Pink
Green
Tall
Stems
Leaves
Petals
Moving
Swinging
Waving
Growing
Blooming
Shadowing
Standing
Playing
Dancing
Strong
Tulips

This kind of writing *seems* innocent, benign. But remember, no text is neutral. Even this text can undergo a deconstruction that peels away layers of power, positioning, and perspective. I didn't challenge Cadence to do so with this text, as it is impossible and not necessarily an aim to have students analyze everything they write. However, as the writer of this book, I want you to realize that these tulips were planted in front of an art museum that Cadence did not know existed until I took the girls' group there to explore visual composition. The manicured landscape around the museum captured Cadence's attention immediately as we drove into the parking lot, mainly because of the stark contrast between the plush museum grounds and the public spaces of St. Francis that had few trees, sparsely planted grass, and no flowers. Questions I could have asked Cadence may have included: Who is this museum for? Who visits the museum? How is the museum funded? Who does not come to the museum and why? Who, then, are the flowers planted for? Why? How does this compare to the parks where you play? Why might there be a difference?

And so on. Cadence could have written a compelling essay for city officials after such an inquiry, but alas, this piece was published as is and not interrogated.

Unlike colorful tulips swaying in the wind, death and dying are topics that many teachers have told me that they would rather children not write about because they're not sure how to "deal" with such pieces. In my experience, however, students have rarely selected a piece on death or dying to make "public" or to publish in some way; therefore, most of this personal writing often remains personal—and private (though this is up to the writer). Every girl wrote about death or dying at one time or another during this study; I include two pieces here that were written as writer's notebook entries by Callie and Sarah at the beginning of second grade.

Grandma

I like my grandma. I care about her because she cares about me. I love her a lot. If she was your grandma, what would you do? Just sit there? You would go do something just like me. I didn't want her to die behind me. If I was there I would tell my family so they would know that she died right there in front of me. That made me sad that she died. I cried all the way home.

I am going to kiss my grandma because it will take away my bad dreams when I'm sleeping. I am going to her funeral to put stuff in her coffin because she is special to me. I hope I will have fun. I am happy to go there. Can you tell me what it is like to be there? I love my grandma very much. I am going to cry on the way there.

I love you grandma.

I want to see you grandma.

She is funny and good to me. OK.

I would like to see her in her coffin. I like her a lot. I hope she still loves me. I can't wait until I get to see her. I love you!

—Callie, written in the autumn of second grade

Callie's narrative about her grandmother's death, the controversial decisions around whether or not children should be present when a death is imminent, the spiritual beliefs around kissing the dead and placing objects in a coffin to accompany a person to another world, and a somewhat unorthodox approach to writing about the dead (I can't wait until I get to see her!) might make some teachers uncomfortable. How do conversations around this piece of writing take place? How will the religious beliefs of the teacher inform the conversation? Of course there are tough, critical questions we could ask about her grandmother's death, particularly since I knew that she was only in her early fifties and had been diagnosed with cancer some time before her death. Are working-class or poor people more prone to getting cancer? Some studies show that St. Francis residents' rates of cancer are higher than any other neighborhood in the metropolitan area due to the polluted natural waterway (a source of water known to be one of the most polluted in the United States), factory emissions, and little access to preventative healthcare. Does Callie know that her grandmother would be considered a very young age in our country to have died? Social class and healthcare issues aside, we could focus on Callie's writing being filled with assumptions around life, death, the place of children during adults' passing, and religion. Though a writing teacher might find this piece a *bit* discomforting, Callie is writing from a Christian perspective that assumes a life beyond earth, and she has written about an older woman who died from (supposed) natural causes—both topics addressed with relative ease by the majority Christian teaching force; and, here Callie incorporates her personal feelings about her grandmother's death, giving a teacher an easy out, so to speak, with regard to encouraging revision and focus.

Sarah incorporates her personal feelings less than Callie. She writes about a sudden death, not one caused by natural aging, but a murder, when her older cousin was shot by his "friends" before his son's first birthday:

Cousins

My cousin died the day before his one-year-old son's birthday. His friends shot him. They didn't want to rob him. He has a daughter, she is five. He had a job. They don't get out no more. They live with their grandma and grandpa. I feel sorry for them. They got a picture only in their room hanging on the wall. They are beautiful. The girl gots curly hair and the boy has short hair.

—Sarah, written in September of second grade

So now we have a second grader narrating a story around her cousin's murder and the resulting lives of two young children. What do writing teachers do with this kind of text? Do we ignore the fact that she is writing about a murder of a young man? Do we ignore the fact that "friends" killing one another for material possessions is not necessarily personal, really, but it may be about doing what is necessary to have objects that carry high status (hooks 1994)? Should we take a look at the abysmal statistics around male youths from working-class and poor homes and their criminal justice system involvement and ask questions about why such boys are too often pushed out of one institution (school) to join another? Or should we think critically about these two young children, the innocent victims left to negotiate life without a father (and perhaps a mother—where is she?). What is the rate of grandparents raising young children—and why? So many important conversations to have . . . my guess is that most people are quite happy to ignore these issues of power, perspective, and positioning, however, to maintain comfort and distance. Instead, what about that curly-haired girl? Could the writer talk more about that? That wouldn't make a lot of sense, would it? Here we have a second grader already thinking about complex issues around murder of parents and the children left to live. Why would she want to describe something as superficial as the curly hair? These stories make us nervous.

And finally, content that might be least appealing to teachers, a piece declaring the hatred the writer feels toward a teacher. In this case, the teacher was me and the writer was Callie. Clearly, Callie was angry and experiencing very strong emotions. As a writer she knew that "anything" was allowed within writing workshop, and she probably felt as if she were pushing the envelope a bit with this entry, knowing that I would be coming around to confer with her:

> I hate you Mrs. Jones. You are mean to me. I am never going to listen to you again. You are mean and a brat. I don't love you any more. I will never make a smile on my face again. I don't love school. I hate school and I hate you.

An energized exchange occurred between Callie and myself around this entry. I applauded her for using writing to tell a story that was important to her, even if that story featured me and my meanness. We also worked through some of what she was angry about, namely the fact that I spent so much time conferring with other writers and, from Callie's perspective, almost no time at all working with her. Nevertheless, this kind of entry is not easy for a teacher to read, and it may be even more difficult to imagine productive conversations occurring around it. But if we keep the tenets and layers of critical literacy in mind, we can understand this text not (only) as a personal attack, but as an attempt to use power, perspective, and positioning to tell a particular story in a way that deconstructs or reconstructs a situation and even works toward social action (she did get my attention, right?).

All writing is allowed. If the writing perpetuates discriminatory practices or stereotypes, then we work diligently toward challenging those notions and reconstructing the texts. One text that was viewed, spoken, and written often was the girl-as-princess-in-need-of-boy-hero narrative. Cultural challenges to this narrative from the perspective of the St. Francis community were necessary; the Princesses in St. Francis section will highlight some of the deconstructive and reconstructive processes and products that were negotiated over time.

Princesses in St. Francis

Princesses of every size, shape, and color filled the classroom on Halloween in second grade. The costume party, a lively and long tradition in St. Francis for both adults and children, brought something to my attention that I had not seriously considered: Princesses in St. Francis were somewhat of an oxymoron that we had not investigated in the classroom. Race, gender, class, and sexuality stereotypes inherent in traditional tales of princesses are always ripe for deconstruction, but particularly for girls living in St. Francis where all of their mothers worked outside of the home and supplied the household with the most stable source of income, while many of the fathers had employment that was much less stable. And one father, Alexis' father, was single and raising four children on his own, managing to find sufficient income sources and juggling the demands of childcare and homemaking. A princess as one-in-waiting for a man who will take her away from household duties and release her from financial stress assumes there are men with access to sufficient financial resources and hired hands to take care of the "dirty" work. In St. Francis, several of the mothers were employed to *do* other people's dirty work: mothers were employed as custodial workers, nursing home aides, and fast food cooks, to name a few.

Drawing on my knowledge of the strength and responsibilities of women in the homes and communities of the girls, we embarked on an inquiry around what it meant to be a girl and a woman in St. Francis, how that was different from perceived lives of "princesses," and ways in which girls were represented in books and films. Books, films, and/or plays that we deconstructed as a group included: *Cinderella, A Little Princess, Whale Rider, Something Beautiful,* and *Junie B. Jones.* Talking around these issues was crucial, and some of the dialogue that ensued from these topics is included throughout this book (particularly in Chapters 8 and 9). Since the focus of this chapter is writing workshop, I will resist the temptation to include transcripts of dialogue that never became written texts in writing workshop, but I am positive that our ongoing dialogues around girls' lives and the representation of girls in texts impacted much of the writing that took place. Sticking to the "princess" theme of this section, the following two written texts reconstruct the typical princess narrative.

The Angel Princess

Once Upon A Time there was an angel princess and her name was [Faith]. She was trapped in a tower and I had to save her because she was my friend.

I saved her from the bad doctor because he was trying to turn her into a monster. If he did turn her into a monster I would miss her because she is my best friend.

To save her I sneaked into the doctor's lab by the window.

> —Rose, written in the spring of second grade

Rose positions herself as the heroine of the story, challenging the notion that all girls wish to be the princess themselves and the stereotype that boys and men occupy positions of heroism. She writes Faith in as the princess, reconstructing the traditional role as reserved for White girls and women, challenging stereotypes around hierarchies of racial status. And finally, Rose includes a male figure who has social status as a "doctor" but is a "bad doctor" trying to turn Rose's friend into a monster (this begs for a critical feminist analysis, but I will move on). Rose, driven by female friendship, puts herself in danger and rescues the Angel Princess from the tower of evil.

Heather writes a very different Princess narrative, but a critically reconstructed one nonetheless:

A Princess

Once upon a time there was a lovely princess. She lived in a castle. She lived with a handsome prince. She had eight children. She was a great cook. Her toilet was running. She wanted to have more kids.

> —Heather, written in the winter of second grade

Heather is the princess of this particular story; she was one of the girls (along with Rose) who dressed up as a princess for Halloween in second grade, and she often pranced around the classroom during choice time creating crowns and wands for herself to use as props in elaborate productions of princess fairytales. Heather's white skin, blonde hair, blue eyes, and petite body aligned with mainstream standards of beauty and those most often representative of princesses in texts, but she reconstructed her narrative to include household chores (such as cooking) and the implied responsibility of childbearing and child rearing. Heather also challenges the traditional fairytale of perfection through including the running toilet, a nuisance to be sure, but certainly a problem Heather is familiar with in her own home. Her inclusion of a "handsome prince" is somewhat arbitrary as he doesn't play a role in the narrative other than simply someone with whom the princess lives. From one perspective, this narrative could be read as the ambitious "lovely" princess who takes care of everything herself *and* has access to a "handsome" male escort when she wants one.

If princess-like looks, attire, and behavior are considered ideal, and prince-like resources assumed to be what girls should aspire to acquiring, girls in St. Francis may find themselves in quite a quandary as readers of such texts and as meaning-makers of their worlds. If they were to judge their family members and other adults within the community based upon the race, gender, and class stereotypes in traditional Princess narratives, they may easily diminish or miss entirely the strong and powerful positions that women occupy in their own homes and across St. Francis, as well as the caretaking roles that men in their families often perform when the mothers are working. In fact, though male power operates dominantly in some spaces of St. Francis (e.g., the corner bar and in drugs and prostitution), the woman—or more specifically, the mother— is positioned as very powerful in private and public spaces. It is the mother (or grandmother) who most often has access to resources inside and outside the community and who occupies positions of official power such as community council president, vice president, and treasurer. It is the mother who interacts most often with institutional bureaucracy (except those of jail and prison) and has learned more of the mainstream language that can open doors of opportunity. All of this, of course, positions the working-poor male problematically in the twenty-first-century labor market, and the effects on his self-esteem and self-worth within a society that still expects that men will be the breadwinners should not be overlooked.

All of this said, an inquiry around princesses and girls' positioning in texts was crucial in the context of St. Francis and the girls' lives. Some of their reconstructions of texts certainly carry the *potential* to challenge the status quo around gender, class, and race relations. At the very least, they are evidence that the girls themselves were thinking critically about such power relations and reworking them in ways that made sense in the present. Some texts, however, are produced with the *intent* that they will be read outside the local context in the hope that some change will take place.

■ Using Our Texts for Social Action: A Plea to Mrs. George W. Bush and a Magazine

In the summer following the girls' second grade year, Laura Bush, the wife of President George W. Bush, visited Bruger Elementary School to talk about literacy. As is the case for many public relations opportunities where journalists will be present to document and represent an event, only a small number of children were selected carefully from the school to be an audience for a read-aloud by Mrs. Bush. None of the girls in this study were selected, but the First Lady's visit did not go unnoticed. Faith, in particular, believed that Mrs. Bush's visit was an opportune time to use text to persuade a person in a powerful position to do something about an injustice in the community. The community swimming pool, located on the playground area of Bruger Elementary School, had two rules that Faith found oppressive: 1—Swimmers had to have their hair checked for lice before entering the pool, and 2—If the swimmer did not have lice, then she or he had to pay $3.00 to enter and swim. Faith wrote the following letter to Mrs. Bush:

> Dear Mrs. Bush,
> Why do the pool at the playground costs three dollars? Why come? Do this—they check [for lice]. If they have lice, then they go home. If they don't have lice, they get in free. You are the First Lady. Please help me.
> Sincerely,
> [Faith]

Faith, not having to worry much about lice infestation (Meyerhoff 2004), decided in her letter that having children subjected to head searches would be reasonable as long as there wasn't a charge for swimming. Faith's focus then is on the social class issue of money and the lack thereof in her home and in the community. On hot summer days this local pool would sometimes have a mere two or three swimmers. Laura Bush never answered Faith, but she had the courage and felt the power to create a text for the purpose of potential social action.

■ A Moment of Satisfaction: Working Toward Social Action Through Publication

Reflecting on that steaming-hot day in June presented at the opening of this chapter, I realize that I was living part of my dream within the space where the girls were constructing a new reality for themselves—writers, photographers, designers, publishers of a magazine—all while thinking carefully and critically about their own gender, class, race, and culturally specific lives. Together we were creating change, even if for just a moment in time, where power relations were turned upside down and the poor, White and African American girls of St. Francis were in charge. This power reversal echoes the empowerment Dorothy Allison writes about as she describes the ways in which writing helped her life seem more real, more tangible—more like the lives she read about in books.

As the girls were constructed as subjects within fluid literacy practices instead of objects within the rigid structures of education, powerful and moving events began to take shape. Being positioned as authors, photographers, reviewers of texts, and publishers of a literary magazine was one such powerful event that served as a reason for celebration in the summer following the girls' second grade school year and can be read as acts of reconstruction and social action.

Introduction to *WINDOWS: a look into a girl's world* . . . [1]

As you read through the selected pages of the magazine presented in this section, imagine hundreds of photographs organized in plastic bins, hundreds of written pages in writers' notebooks sprawled on tables, and dozens of books with carefully placed sticky notes marking passages, connections, and possible topics for discussion. The publication of this magazine was miraculously pulled together in a three-week time period during our summer program. But the language- and literacy-based preparation was at least two years of engaged dialogue, reading, writing, and photographing practices inside and outside the classroom. The girls had far too much writing to represent in a single issue, and their decision-making processes around what to include in the magazine were sometimes stressful, and on occasion even created riffs in our publishing community. But in the end, we survived as a group and held a grand celebratory exhibition, inviting families, community members, teachers, university representatives, and city leaders to view our work—all of whom were genuinely impressed with the girls' poise and knowledge as they spoke about the processes of creating a magazine from the ground up.

WINDOWS: a look into a girl's world . . . is the title created by the girls during a study of metaphor in the summer following their second grade year. We explored window as a metaphor for life in St. Francis: the multiple shapes lives take on, the different ways lives are lived, and the ways in which people let others into their lives or keep them out. Figure 11–1 shows the cover of the magazine and is followed by select pages.

▪ Reading the Magazine: Reconstruction and Social Action

Like Dorothy Allison, the girls and women in St. Francis rarely saw representations of their lived realities in literary texts. In *Fire* by Cadence, *My Brother* and *Window to Flaming Hots* by Rose, and *The Window* by Joanie, the girls have told stories about their lives and taken accompanying photographs to visually represent their experiences. Wendy Ewald put it well in the quote that helps to frame this chapter when she stated that the photographs and written texts constructed by the children could not necessarily convey the difficulty of a situation, but they are beginning points for making some kind of sense of lived realities. I would add that part of this sense-making was also coming to at least a temporary belief that their situations are "fine" the way they were, using Joanie's ending in *The Window*. As my mom might say, "It is what it is,"

FIG. 11–1. Student-created magazine. The cover appears first, followed by select pages.

Fire

My house caught on fire, but our house on the first floor did not catch on fire. It was the 2nd floor that caught on fire.

My sister was about to get in the tub. I just got out from the tub. My hair was soaked from the hot steaming shower.

Windows, June 2003

As all of us came rushing out of the house my step dad told us to walk. I guess he is stupid. My mom was scared to death. I was too—for my hamster. I thought she was going to die.

We asked the firemen if we had to move because the top floor roof was about to collapse. We called the firemen and asked if we could stay at a hotel for a while.

Then the firemen called the Red Cross to give us some clothes. It was a sweatshirt and sweat pants. We took them to wear.

My grandma and grandpa were there to take us to the hotel. It is downtown. It took an hour or two. To get to the hotel you have to go across the viaduct. It scares me a lot. To get to school we take the bus or walk. That is hard because I eat at the hotel and that filled me up and my tummy hurt. When I was walking it slowed me down. When I was going to school it hurt. We met my teacher. Her name is Mrs. Jones.

FIG. 11–1 (*continued*)

Smoking

A girl asked me if she could see my camera. I said yes. She took a picture of this young boy smoking, but he didn't smile.

I think that he should not smoke because he is not grown yet and his lungs can get black. His heart can also turn black. He cannot live if he smokes. Nobody should do that.

I looked at TV and somebody's father died. He died because he was smoking. That's why you and your kids shouldn't do it.

Somebody is telling your kids to smoke. Sometimes they say, "Can I go to the store?"

The boy or girl at the store say, "You can't get that."

Then they say it's for my mom or dad and they smoke.

You should talk about that with your kids. If they say no, they don't smoke, watch them. If they say yes, you have to try to get them to stop. Still watch them because they still will smoke.

Book Review

Powerpuff Professor

In this first chapter book of the Powerpuff Girls series, Professor Utonium becomes a superhero. He wants the Powerpuff Girls to be safe when they're fighting and he starts fighting for them so they don't get hurt. At the end he let them fight alone because he wasn't good at being a super-hero. He wanted to be an ordinary person. All kinds of girls will like this book, especially girls who are strong and independent.

My Brother Austin

My brother Austin fell out of the 3rd floor window, but he is okay. He fell out because he leaned back on the screen. He went to the doctor. She said he is okay to go home.

Me and my mom and my dad cleaned up the trash so he can come home. He came home but I have to play with him safely because he is sore.

When he is healed, I will play with him all spring break and on Saturdays and Sundays. But sometimes I can't because sometimes I get in trouble.

Windows, June 2003

FIG. 11–1 (*continued*)

Window to Flaming Hots

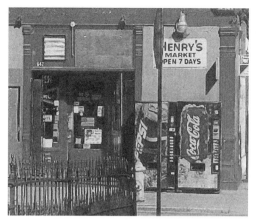

"Window to Flaming Hots"

The window is a door—and this door leads into a special place for me. This place has stuff for me. It has chips for me. Flaming Hots are crunchy, tasty, and hot. Flaming Hots are the same color as Henry's. When I walk down to Henry's I think of Flaming Hots. And Flaming Hots are my favorite.

I Was So Mad!

I was feeling upset
because I was so mad!
I was stomping my
    feet on the floor!
I was yelling every word.
I was not paying attention
    to Ms. Jones!
I was not writing in my
    writer's notebook!
But then I just started
    to write, write, write
    away and I was so
    happy!

Windows, June 2003

My Rich Grandma

My grandma is rich because my other grandma gives her money to my Rich grandma. She gave me ten dollars. I was holding her hand and I was scared because she might fall.

She walked me to the front room. She had a lock on the door so nobody would get in the room.

I saw a treasure box.

I got ten dollars out of the box.

FIG. 11–1 (*continued*)

Art Museum

I like the museum because there were angels that looked like a person. There was a white statue of a woman who had white wings. I thought it was beautiful because the artist put light white on the body and dark white on the wings.

I also saw a man. It looked like the artist made him with clay but the color was white. His butt was showing. His leg was broken off. His arm was broken too. I thought it was funny that his butt was showing, but then I learned that the artist wanted to show it.

I also saw a woman ballet dancer. Her leg was kicked out front.

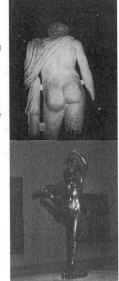

All through the museum there were pictures that tell you stories about each piece of art.

The green room looked pretty. They have pictures with flowers on them with many colors. I didn't know which one to pick to write about because they were all beautiful. One was a rose and the other was too, but it was a different color.

I would recommend that everyone go to the museum because you can look at all of the art. You can also bring cameras and a writer's notebook to help you remember all the details of what the artists made.

The Window

I took a picture of this window because it is broken and I have a broken window at my apartment too. It's in my hallway. Now we have a board on it like a stop sign.

My window is not the same shape as the one in the picture— my window is shaped like a hexagon. My window does not have a cup in it either. This window looks just fine on this blue house.

Windows, June 2003

FIG. 11–1 (*continued*)

or "You have to work with what you've got." Placing the narratives written by the girls in a public space, such as this magazine, challenges the assumption that only some (privileged) lives have the right to be written, published, and read.

Some of the texts were essays written about places outside the community that we visited as a group. *Art Museum* by Faith is one of those essays, and it focused on Faith's observations of various pieces of artwork in the museum, her wonder around some of them, and her recommendation that visiting the museum is something that everyone should do. Deciding to include this particular piece in the magazine was interesting since so few people in St. Francis feel comfortable entering such "high fallutin'" places like an art museum. However, Faith is reconstructing the assumption that public art spaces are for privileged citizens and should, instead, be considered to be for everyone.

Powerpuff Professor is a book review written by Rose. The series of books is about three young girl superheroes. The book itself challenges some assumptions around gender and who can perform superheroic identities, and Rose taps into this reconstruction of typically male-dominated book characters. She ends her review with, "All kinds of girls will like this book, especially girls who are strong and independent." Like her princess narrative where Rose is the heroine, the Powerpuff Girls continue to aid Rose in the reconstruction of girls as strong, independent, and heroic.

And finally, *Smoking*, an essay by Faith on underage smoking in St. Francis that was triggered by Faith's friend taking a photograph of a ten-year-old boy with a cigarette in his hand. Faith pulls together her knowledge of smoking and health-related issues from television, her understanding of the common practice of children buying cigarettes at the corner stores for their parents, and her belief that parents talking to their kids will make a difference in their children's decision making.

In all, the magazine combined stories about girls' lives, reconstructed texts around gender stereotypes, persuasive essays calling for social action in the community, and introductions to places outside the community. Because of its publication and the popularity of this magazine within the families and across the community (it is the one thing Cadence's mother asked me to mail to her when she was in jail for three months during Cadence's third grade year), this text serves as social action—changing the face of what is published and what is read. But it is also working toward social action on a more personal level, geared toward the lives of the girls who produced it.

◾ Reading the Magazine as Social Action in the Lives of Eight Girls

Within the framework of critical literacy, a young preadolescent girl can begin shaping new identities that add at least a second possibility to the mothering desire as described in Chapters 8 and 9. Narratives that are produced on the margins of dominant discourses, and from the margins of normalized experiences are powerful vehicles of agency inside and outside of school. Such narrative productions challenge dominant discourses because they insert alternative realities to be read (or heard) and considered by others while opening up spaces where the writer/speaker can position herself in productive ways (Dyson 2001; Lankshear and Knoebel 2002; Sahni 2001; Wortham 2001). Perhaps if young Callie begins to perceive herself as a producer of knowledge, a writer, a photographer, a journalist even, she will have life-oriented dreams for fulfillment outside of or in combination with a mothering identity, which could lead to financial stability. This financial stability and career fulfillment could potentially better prepare Callie for caring for her children if, and when, she decides to have them after she has "waited" (as her mother urged her to do). Just waiting, however, is not a viable solution. If Callie and the other girls are not constructing identities and building solid abilities to position themselves well in the workforce, the waiting may prevent some physical challenges during teenage pregnancy and birth, but it will not prevent the long, hard road of raising children on a minimum-wage income.

The magazine is an example of a multifaceted, technologically influenced literacy project that positions young girls as agents within an educational endeavor. Continued over longer periods of time, the possibilities of such an ongoing project are endless—but even with only one issue under their belt, the girls built confidence in their abilities as photographers, writers, digital masters, readers, and designers. Publishing a single issue of a magazine, however, wouldn't have had near the impact if it had not been for the long-term relationship building, deep understandings of community and home lives, and the day-to-day work we conducted together in the regular classroom and after school. Though it looks like (and is) an impressive piece of work—such a piece of work could have been accomplished in a very short period of time without all of the other understandings. My belief is that such work then loses much value and sustaining power.

◾ Critical Literacy and the Writing Workshop

Textual practices in the writing workshop are never neutral, innocent, or benign. Assuming this as fact, why not purposefully engage the construction and reconstruction of texts to work toward social justice and action? In this chapter I have presented three goals that I have in a writing workshop: allowing all topics, using knowledge about students' lives to help construct and reconstruct texts, and encouraging the use of texts for social action. This kind of critically focused work is deeply rooted in the lives of the students, as I have analyzed here, and grows critical literacy practices out of children's and families' cultural ways of being.

Exercise 11.1 Thinking Critically About the Writing Workshop

Consider the following about your writing workshop:

- How are students positioned in writing workshop by you, the teacher? By other students?

- Which positions are productive? Counterproductive?

- Do students' texts ever perpetuate damaging stereotypes?

- How can a critical literacy perspective help writers reconsider how and why they write texts?

Note

1   The publishing of this magazine was funded by the Martha Holden Jennings Foundation, funding secured by Deborah Hicks. Karen Spector worked tirelessly with our group and on her own to turn the visions of the girls' designs into reality through technology.

12

Windows of Opportunity
Critical Work in School and Society

L ike this book, my understandings of literacy in the classroom weave between students' lives, theory, my knowledge of the community, my personal experiences, literacy research, students' families, my critique of social stratification, and contemporary events. There is no linear path to critical literacy practices nor is there a linear path for our students' literacy development; these paths are continuously changing as they are informed by our readings of words and the world around us. This chapter will weave together, once again, the fabrics of life, literacy, identity, St. Francis, social critique, and the girls and their mothers to create a complex picture of our future work, beginning with revisiting my opening narrative in Chapter 1.

My conscious awareness of social class was set in motion in fourth grade when I stepped out of our van and stared in awe at Mrs. Stritt's middle-class brick home in suburbia. Since then my awareness has continued to be heightened and my tolerance for classist remarks, judgments, and behaviors has decreased considerably. I find myself in a precarious position, however, as I stand with one foot in a privileged middle-class world and the other in a world of working-class and poor people that is fraught with daily struggles. Who am I? I often ask myself this strange question, answering it differently each time. This is only the tip of the iceberg when it comes to the complicated nature of transcending social class boundaries, with my journey starting in school where I first encountered middle-class others and felt that I should discard the parts of me that didn't seem to "fit" with what I saw others doing. Because I was sometimes able to blend in with a middle-class crowd through the performance of an identity that felt very foreign, my efforts to leave behind the rough-around-the-edges parts of me were somewhat fruitful.

But alas, my struggle in adulthood has been to regain those very parts, to sink into them and to be caressed by them and their familiarity and security, to embrace and combine them with other identities I have shaped across time and place. Today my fear is not that a middle-class acquaintance will get a glimpse of my working-poor roots, it is that my poor and working-class relatives, friends, and acquaintances will view me as different from them, as some kind of a sellout, or worse, as someone who possesses much book knowledge but very little common sense and hands-on experience. This fear was confirmed in a dream I had during the writing of this book, a dream that I will represent here knowing that the effect cannot be conveyed in words.

My starched, white blouse crinkles as I pile platters around a circular tray at my waist, tipping a stone-colored dinner plate allowing the gravy to ooze toward the potatoes and away from the edge. With the platters carefully balanced, I spread my left fingers wide on the bottom, stretch and brace my hand, and thrust my left arm above my head with ease. Weaving through the crowded kitchen area, the tray begins to wobble and tip. Surprised, I quickly rotate my hand and carefully rest the collection of dinners near my waist. It is like this that I hesitantly made my way to the table filled with a White, chatty family awaiting their evening meal.

Back in the servers' section, I absentmindedly shove a fork and knife together and wrap them tightly in a square cotton napkin. Then I panic, and out of the corner of my eye I see a lone chicken breast on the grill—could it belong to my table?

Oh no.

It's *my* job to check orders.

Did I miss one?

Rushing back to the only table that is my responsibility, careful on the slick grease-covered floor, I am met with angry glares. One woman has nothing in front of her, everyone else has finished eating and the table is piled high with dirty plates, bowls, and glasses. That dark-headed woman stared at me in disgust, nostrils flaring, lips pursed, eyes nearly closed, head shaking slowly from side to side.

Oh no.

She didn't want her meal, she just wanted to get *out* of this *place*. The contempt in her voice landed in my throat. I couldn't speak, walk, or move. I just looked at her.

Voices from the kitchen broke my trance and I realized that the really disgusted, mean, hurtful woman in front of me wasn't the only one after my dignity, the cooks were yelling, "Who's the dumb ass that left this chicken dinner here?" As if in slow motion I turned toward the kitchen, the family paraded past me huffing, and when I managed to look back at the empty table all I could see was the tip: nothing.

I really needed the money too.

Spit was flying out of the gray-haired man's mouth as he ran toward me with wild eyes, cash register and door keys jingling frantically as he punched the air to emphasize each syllable:

"What is *wrong* with you!"

It wasn't a question. It was a statement. He knew I was inept; he knew it was a mistake to hire me. He knew I couldn't do this job, that I wasn't thinking in the many ways servers need to be thinking. I wasn't strategizing, I wasn't checking with my customers, I wasn't scanning the place constantly to see what needed to be done, to solve the long list of problems always facing workers in a restaurant.

He knew it.

I knew it.

With flooding eyes and a quivering chin, I defended myself the best way I knew, shouting through saliva and wiping my running nose:

"I'm a Pro-*fes*-sor! What do you *expect*!"

Then I woke up, heart pounding, fists clenched, and thanking God it was only a dream as I tried to calm myself beneath the tink-ta-tink of raindrops on a tin roof in Louisiana, while reflecting back on my years as a server and everything that used to come so naturally to me.

■ At Home in Louisiana: A Working-Class Paradise

My mom moved to Shreveport, Louisiana in 2004 to work in a General Motors' automotive factory on the assembly line. The Ohio plant she had worked in prior to her move was facing more layoffs and rumor had it that there would be a lockout: an unannounced closing of the plant and lost jobs. Mom couldn't afford to lose her job just yet, and when she read an announcement that cash bonuses were being offered for anyone willing to build the Hummer3 in Shreveport she submitted her name. Two weeks later it was a done deal, she packed up some bags and drove south on a Friday, slated to begin work on Monday. That same year I moved from Cincinnati, Ohio to New York City to begin a position as an assistant professor at Teachers College, Columbia University.

Mom bought a two-bedroom trailer in a park outside of town and filled it with wind chimes, plants, books, candles, floral furniture, and the smells of her cooking—I couldn't wait to get there. In the summer of 2005 my three-year-old daughter and I spent a week in Shreveport and fell comfortably into the community: swimming at the park pool, playing with kids, chatting with parents, and riding scooters on the yellow speed-bumped black-topped streets. I must admit that I was more than proud when neighbors at the pool would wave and ask when we moved in. "Just visiting my mom this week," I would respond. No talk about New York City or what I did for a living—and no questions. It was better than nice; it felt like paradise. The older kids added to my comfort; just like my brother and I had so long ago in rural Ohio, the kids ruled the trailer park. I felt very much at home.

It was there in that modest setting in the rural South where this horrifying dream disturbed my sleep, and later, my wide-awake days.

Unlike my mother, I don't usually attempt dream interpretation but this one lit my pants on fire and demanded attention. Two major fears became evident:

1. My fear of losing the intelligences and practices honed as a working-class/poor girl coming of age as a server.
2. My fear of being perceived as incompetent by working-class people, that they might see me as a "waste of skin and bones."

The rest of this chapter focuses on four interrelated issues that I hope you, the reader, will come away from this book with:

- Assumptions and stereotypes grounded in social class are uninformed, perpetuated through the construction of texts of all sorts, and are in desperate need of being deconstructed and reconstructed.

- Challenging stereotypes and learning about (and from) individual children and families is an imperative piece of any educational practice grounded in social justice.

- Serious consideration of the identity work students must negotiate if they take different paths from family members is crucial.

- Critical literacy offers tools for becoming more "socially-perceptive" (Gee 2001) and equipping oneself with the skills necessary to work toward social change; teachers and children alike should be actively engaged in critical literacy practices.

▪ The Workers of St. Francis: Intelligence and Judgment

Think back to the chapters in this book that described St. Francis, the history of some of the residents, and occupations held by some of the mothers and fathers of the girls in this study: custodial work, nursing home aide work, fast food service work, bank clerical work, retail work, handyman work, house painting, and so on were all represented. Much of these blue collar or pink collar positions are assumed to be filled by "unskilled" workers who are replaceable and interchangeable. Anyone who does such work or lives with someone who does, however, knows that this is simply not true, that tremendous intelligence is necessary for each position.[1] In an impressive study of blue-collar workers on the job, Mike Rose reminds us simply that "To work is to solve problems" (2004, 200). Rose documented sophisticated perception, improvisation, troubleshooting, memory, self-observation, use of tools, modification of activity, split-second decision making, and ongoing alterations of even "mastered" activities to increase safety and effectiveness in waitresses, plumbers, hairstylists, carpenters, welders, and electrical workers. Unskilled? Not quite.

So, why are such large groups of workers assumed to be less intelligent, less worthy of health benefits, retirement funds, living wages, respect? Rose (2004) recalls that throughout U.S. history, most forms of work that were previously unprecedented, factory work during the industrial revolution for example, came to be perceived as more valuable than the work that had already been in existence. In our current information-driven craze, value is placed on technological workers and the "intelligence" necessary for such positions. But can we survive without sanitation workers, nursing home workers, custodians, roofers, hairstylists, restaurant servers, auto mechanics, painters, road workers, childcare providers? If the answer is the likely "no" then why is it that social value for such positions is not greater? Our definitions of intelligence, "smart," success, and skill are in need of reworking.

These workers were the parents, grandparents, aunts, and uncles of the children in St. Francis. They are problem solvers. They are perceptive. And, like their children, they are always reading between the lines. How will they read you? Let's hope they read that you respect them; that you believe they are intelligent and capable, and that you are treating them the way you would want to be treated by the teachers of your children if you have them. Most importantly, let them see that the curriculum engagements you immerse their children in are rich and meaningful, the same kind of relevant and empowering education you wish you had had yourself and that you believe is imperative for every child in our country.

Before moving on, I want you to reflect on your own position as an educator.

When are you respected for what you do? When do you sense that someone doesn't value the intelligence, practices, and complex cognitive work involved in your day-to-day activities? The ol' saying that "Those who can't, teach" has not been deleted from cultural memory or mainstream belief. So what are the specialized skills, dispositions, practices, and knowledge bases that inform your work? Why wouldn't the same be true of any occupation? A quote from Mike Rose's book is apt here:

> Judgments about intelligence carry great weight in our culture, and one of the ways we judge each other's intelligence is through the work we do. There are many distinctions that can be made among types of work, distinctions related to income, autonomy, cleanliness, physical risk, and so on. These have a harshly real material meaning, but carry symbolic meaning as well. There's a moral and characterological aura to occupational autonomy, income, cleanliness, leading us to slip from qualities of the *work* to qualities of the *worker.* (Emphasis added, 2004, xxi)

Challenging stereotypes grounded in social class and the "work" someone does is an important step toward valuing all lives, appreciating the intelligences of everyone, and envisioning the important academic work that can be done to enhance and extend literacy practices already being performed by students and families as they negotiate their worlds.

▥ Mothers, Jail, and Princesses with Running Toilets: Teachers as Learners

I couldn't have known the impact that the girls' relationships with their mothers might have had on their engagements with school and literacy before carefully studying their writing and oral conversations. I wouldn't have known to ask mothers and grandmothers what their wishes were for their precious daughters before noticing that several had informally said to me they hope their daughter waits to have children. I couldn't have realized the intimate relationships children had with the concept of jail and the constant threat of police officers taking someone away until attending community meetings, talking with neighborhood adults, and opening a classroom space where such conversations could take place. I wouldn't have known that stereotypical versions of femininity and masculinity or typical male and female roles were not necessarily the "truth" in St. Francis homes before I spent time visiting families and foregrounding gender in our curricular work together. And I could never have realized that a second grade girl could so eloquently combine her desire to be treated with respect (princess) with her knowledge about childcare and housework, her value in being independent, and her contentment with living a dream within an imperfect material reality (running toilet) before engaging students in critical readings of some of their favorite things: princesses, gendered relationships, and expressions of idealistic versions of motherhood.

The girls and their families were my teachers, they taught me about assumptions, stereotypes, strength, and resiliency. I took what I learned and considered how to use it to better understand students in the classroom, their relationships with me and with one another, their connections or disconnections with academic curricula, and the ways their identities were being shaped inside and outside school. I also strategically molded it into literacy engagements of all sorts: films, books, magazines, photography, conversations. The critical perspective I carried with me into my work with the girls was grounded in the assumption that all texts were constructed and therefore could be deconstructed and reconstructed toward social justice. As a result of this perspective, everything I learned about the children, families, and community helped me to anticipate what kinds of deconstructions would make sense to the young literacy learners. I also planned rich opportunities to reconstruct, by foregrounding the perspectives of the girls who had for so long been missing from the mainstream texts they read in their worlds of home and school.

We must learn from those whose best interests we are supposed to serve. How could we possibly teach any other way? We must engage our own critical literacy practices to reflect on perspective, positioning, and power within the curriculum and "methods" we use to engage students in our classrooms. Many well-intended teachers don't consider children's complex histories and identities because they assume that a goal in education is to "lift" those children "up" and away from community practices that reflect working-class or poor lives. Please reconsider this. I can only speak for myself as someone who has traversed the social class divide, but I still experience great pain and ambiguity around the decisions I have made that have carried me farther and farther from who I consider an important part of the "real me" and from those I love the most (remember the horrifying dream?). It takes a great deal of effort to maintain two lives that seem to be separated by an entire universe. This effort, for me, is not only physical and social in the sense that I travel a great deal to be with my family, but it is painfully psychological; I am always afraid of not being accepted or valued by those I most respect and admire. This difficult identity work may never be completely prevented or avoided, but careful and sensitive treatment of such precarious issues is not beyond the scope of the work of a school or classroom. Personally, preserving the part of me who is the girl who grew up poor with strong, independent working-class women and engaging, sensitive working-class men is the most important work I do. It is not, however, a message that I received in school; a message that relationships and identities are important and not to be shed in the process of academic achievement and class mobility. Perhaps if we begin with what we learn is most important to our students, and for many that would mean family relations and community, we can pave a road toward school success that does not assume getting "up and out" of communities where we feel most at home.

◼ Not Just Academics: Critical Literacy and Our World

At first glance critical literacies may seem appropriately embedded in academic practice within schools—the concept looks great, sounds great, and offers a fresh, critical perspective on reading, writing, and talking in literacy classrooms. But we are a people who tend to make judgments, assumptions, and perpetuate stereotypes, and immersion in critical literacy can help us change these practices. Gee (2001) offers the term "socially-perceptive" literacy as congruent with critical literacy arguing that this critical perspective can offer us much-needed insight into social relations, oral conversations, and group dynamics. Gee believes that socially-perceptive/critical literacy can help us to consider identities and the ways in which they are performed in social interactions (remember the jail chapter, mothering chapters, and the teacher-as-a-threat chapter). By critically considering such important things, we make decisions about how to position ourselves (as educators) within an interaction, what we might say, and how we might say it to not position ourselves as superior to families and children.

Critical literacy, then, is not just another way to *do* reading and writing, but it is a way of perceiving the world around us and using our power to work toward social justice. How I wish I would have been engaged in such ways as a young student! As someone who was usually on the margins of mainstream society through childhood and adolescence, I felt quite powerful when first introduced to critical literacy as a graduate student. The girls in this book often felt powerful as well. They learned to reconsider surface meanings and question texts, rethink their own stereotypes around class, race, and gender, and proudly present experiences that were "normal" to them and in contrast to what is too often portrayed as normal in our society.

◼ The Work Ahead of Us: Making a Difference in Society and in Schools

I wish I could believe that the work we do in schools would, indeed, *save* the world. But it won't. Throughout this book I have urged you to think about yourself, students, families, literacy, and society in particular ways that *can* make a difference in how people perceive and value one another. Critically focused work *will* make a difference in students' lives as they read the world through different lenses and challenge systems that marginalize them and their families. This work will *absolutely* make a difference in your role as an educator and in your everyday experiences. But what I have proposed in this book will not change the structures of our society unless we address the systemic social, economic, and political inequities in our country. Relying on the writing of Berliner (2005) and Rothstein (2004), I will lay out some ideas to consider.

In a moving and motivating essay David Berliner (2005) dismisses the view of school reform as something that happens inside schools. Berliner considers contemporary views of school reform as "impoverished" and argues that the assumption that changing schools will cure society's ails is absurd. And it is. Poverty, the social, economic, and political problem that Berliner calls the unexamined 600-pound gorilla in the classroom, is where our focus should be.

The gap between the rich and the poor has continued to widen, not narrow, in the past twenty years, and we find ourselves in a place where the state of Michigan alone has lost 130,000 jobs in recent years due to General Motors cutbacks, with GM recently announcing 30,000 more employees to be cut nationwide by 2008; where trade unions—organizations that have protected working-class men and women for decades—are being dismantled; where politics aligns itself with corporate capital eroding public space and social support systems (Giroux 2004); where neoliberal capitalism stretches its tentacles across the globe for cheaper labor and wealthier consumers (McLaren 2006); where we are on the brink of a healthcare crisis and beyond crisis in the fight for democratically run public schools; and where we incarcerate our citizens at rates exceptionally higher than any other country in the world (International Centre for Prison Studies). Those carrying the burden of such social, political, and economic shifts are those who have always suffered most in our country's history. Social class matters, and its oppressive forces will matter more to all of us as time moves on.

Richard Rothstein (2004) offers some insights into the "problem" of social class within educational institutions. Rothstein's sophisticated analysis argues that closing the achievement gap between White students and Black students, based on test scores, will not close the social, economic, and political gaps between middle-class and poor children and adults in U.S. society. Rothstein points out that at least as important as broad and sweeping school reform is the need for social and economic policies that address persistent and perpetuating inequities. Rothstein writes:

Along with efforts to improve school practices, educators, like students they try to prepare, should exercise their own rights and responsibilities of citizenship to participate in redressing the inequalities with which children come to school. (129)

Areas of concern for Rothstein include the fact that income in the United States is more unequal and working-class families have "less access to medical care here than in any other industrial nation" (129); that fifty years after the Supreme Court's decision on desegregation schools are radically segregated by race and social class in the United States; and that academic achievement of poor children declines severely when a school's free and reduced lunch rate surpasses 40 percent of the school population.

Rothstein further argues that "for lower-class families, low wages for working parents with children, poor health care, inadequate housing, and lack of opportunity for high-quality early childhood, after-school and summer activities are all educational problems" (130). I would add to this long list that incarceration of parents and the over-surveillance of working-class and poor neighborhoods by the criminal justice system is also an educational problem affecting millions of students each day.

As active citizens in a democracy, educators can exercise their voters' rights by demanding that housing, development, zoning, transportation, and other policies providing the framework for those who live there be changed to encourage social class integration in society and schools. And given Rothstein's statement that making policy to narrow the income gap could be the most important step toward equity in education, it would make sense that we band together and push for living wages for all workers.

In concluding his book, Rothstein writes:

> What this book has tried to show is that eliminating the social class differences in student outcomes requires eliminating the impact of social class on children in American society. It requires abandoning the illusion that school reform alone can save us from having to make the difficult economic and political decisions that the goal of equality inevitably entails. School improvement does have an important role to play, but it cannot shoulder the entire burden, or even most of it, on its own. (149)

So here, in this book, I have tried to imagine what some version of in-school reform might entail. This reform would be based on deep social and historical understandings of ourselves and the families and communities with which we work; a critical perspective toward power, positioning, and perspective; and a curricular framework grounded in deconstruction, reconstruction, and social action.

This kind of reform will help us do the "dirty work," you might say, to dig in the trenches with one child or her father to build new understandings about one another and new possibilities for our futures. However, more reform is necessary to get the job done—the kind that gets negotiated in sanitized spaces with formal protocols and lots of people in suits. But we can also push that work forward by contacting our local, state, and national officials and demanding social and economic policies that reflect the equity we work for every day in our classrooms. Let them know that we bear witness to the radical and detrimental effects of social class marginalization on children each day, and that we understand this to be a societal issue and not one that is born within individual children or their families.

It's a Tall Order, I know. Teachers, future teachers, and graduate students with whom I work often sit with wide eyes, nodding their heads up and down in agreement, getting fired up about researching a community, learning from families, building critical literacy practices out of everyday lives, and being active citizens in the thrust toward a more just society. Then we get to the planning part of this work and people cast their eyes downward and speak in small voices. The common sentiment becomes impossibility: time, institutional responsibilities, curricular mandates, high-stakes testing, families' schedules, and so forth. For every suggestion there are five excuses for why it *just won't work*. Here I encourage you to start small, dear friend. Choose one section of the research exercise in Chapter 2 as a focus across a semester and work outwards from there; begin with one student or family who seems least connected with school and learn from them first; pick up a favorite book and read it critically considering perspective, positioning, and power, and then use it in a different way with your class; audiotape your small group and one-on-one reading or writing conferences for a day and analyze them through a critical literacy lens; contact your representatives in the Senate or House about one issue that is important to you; send emails to friends and families about the importance of social policy to educational reform. Do one tiny thing. And then do another. And another. And suddenly you will find yourself habitually reading and rewriting the world in new and powerful ways—but the first step must be taken.

Perhaps the most important lesson that I have learned from the children and families in St. Francis (and from my family as well) is that opportunity doesn't just come knockin' at your door. If you want something to happen you do what it takes, scrimping and scraping all along the way. Apathy doesn't help you get the next meal on the table, the rent paid, and the kids to school in the morning, but pushing forward when many obstacles are blocking your path does. So I will end my thoughts, for now, with a photograph taken by Faith and her accompanying caption that I read as a challenge to us all in our march toward social justice:

Cut Out Your Own Windows of Opportunity

▨ Note

1   See Barbara Ehrenreich's book *Nickel and Dimed: On (Not) Getting By in America* for an engaging read on pink collar low-wage work and workers.

References

Allard, H., and J. Marshall. 1985. *Miss Nelson Is Missing*. New York: Houghton Mifflin.

Allen, J. B., ed. 1999. *Class Actions: Teaching for Social Justice in Elementary and Middle School*. New York: Teachers College Press.

Allison, D. 1988, 2002. *Trash*. Ithaca, NY: Firebrand Books.

———. 2001. A Question of Class. In *Growing up Poor: A Literary Anthology,* ed. R. Coles, R. Testa, and M. Coles, 75–86. New York: New Press.

Alvermann, D., J. Moon, and M. Hagood. 1999. *Popular Culture in the Classroom: Teaching and Researching Critical Media Literacy*. Newark, DE: International Reading Association.

Alvermann, D., and S. Hong Xu. 2003. "Children's Everyday Literacies: Intersections of Popular Culture and Language Arts Instruction." *Language Arts* 81:145–54.

Anzaldua, G. 1993. La conciencia de la mestiza: Towards a New Consciousness. In *American Feminist Thought at Century's End: A Reader*, ed. L. Kauffman, 427–40. Cambridge, MA: Blackwell.

———. 1999. *Borderlands/La frontera*. San Francisco: Aunt Lute Books.

Atwell, N. 1998. *In the Middle: New Understandings About Writing, Reading, and Learning*. Portsmouth, NH: Heinemann.

Bakhtin, M. M. 1981. *The Dialogic Imagination: Four Essays by M. M. Bakhtin*. Austin, TX: University of Texas Press.

———. 1990. *Art and Answerability: Early Philosophical Essays*. Austin, TX: University of Texas Press.

———. 1993. *Toward a Philosophy of the Act*. Austin, TX: University of Texas Press.

Barton, D., and M. Hamilton. 1998. *Local Literacies*. New York: Routledge.

Bell, B., J. Gaventa, and J. Peters, eds. 1990. *We Make the Road by Walking: Myles Horton and Paulo Freire (Conversations on Education and Social Change)*. Philadelphia: Temple University Press.

Berliner, D. 2005. "Our Impoverished View of Educational Reform." *Teachers College Record*. Retrieved at www.tcrecord.org/content.asp?contentid=12106.

Bernstein, B. 1971. *Class, Codes, and Control: Theoretical Studies Towards a Sociology of Language*. New York: Schocken Books.

Bigelow, B. 2005. "The Recruitment Minefield: Critical Literacy Activities Can Protect Students Against Predatory Military Recruiting." *Rethinking Schools* 19(3): 42–48.

Bomer, R., and K. Bomer. 2001. *For a Better World: Reading and Writing for Social Action*. Portsmouth, NH: Heinemann.

Bourdieu, P. 1991. *Language and Symbolic Power*. Cambridge, MA: Harvard University Press.

———. 1992. *Language and Symbolic Power*. Cambridge, MA: Polity Press.

———. 1994. Structures, Habitus, Power: Basis for a Theory of Symbolic Power. In *Culture, Power, History: A Reader in Contemporary Social Theory*, ed. N. Dirks, G. Eley, and S. Ortner, 155–99. Princeton, NJ: Princeton University Press.

Bowman, M. 2006. "America's Undocumented Population Grows." *Voice of America*. Retrieved at www.voanews.com/english/archive/2006-03/2006-03-07-voa75.cfm?CFID=5787475&CFTOKEN=99915701.

Calkins, L. M. 1994. *The Art of Teaching Writing*. Portsmouth, NH: Heinemann.

———. 2001. *The Art of Teaching Reading*. Portsmouth, NH: Heinemann.

Child Welfare League of America. *Federal resource center for children of prisoners*. Retrieved on May 24, 2006, from www.cwla.org/programs/incarcerated/cop _factsheet.htm.

Christensen, L. 2000. *Reading, Writing and Rising Up: Teaching About Social Justice and the Power of the Written Word*. Milwaukee, WI: Rethinking Schools.

Cisneros, S. 2001. *The House on Mango Street*. In *Growing up Poor: A Literary Anthology*, ed. R. Coles and R. Testa, 26–35. New York: New Press.

Clarke, L. 2005. "'A Stereotype Is Something You Listen to Music on': Navigating a Critical Curriculum." *Language Arts* 83(2): 147–58.

Coles, R., and R. Testa, eds. 2001. *Growing up Poor: A Literary Anthology*. New York: New Press.

Collins, P. H. 1994. Shifting the Center: Race, Class, and Feminist Theorizing About Motherhood. In *Mothering: Ideology, Experience, and Agency*, ed. E. N. Glenn, G. Change, and L. R. Forcey, 45–66. New York: Routledge.

Comber, B. 1998. Critical Literacy: What's It All About? *Education Matters* 3(3): 9–14.

———. 2001a. Classroom Explorations in Critical Literacy. In *Critical Literacy: A Collection of Articles from the Australian Literacy Educators' Association*, ed. H. Fehring and P. Green, 90–102. Newark, DE: International Reading Association.

———. 2001b. Critical Literacies and Local Action: Teacher Knowledge and a "New" Research Agenda. In *Negotiating Critical Literacies in Classrooms*, ed. B. Comber and A. Simpson, 271–82. Mahwah, NJ: Lawrence Erlbaum Associates.

———. 2002. "Critical Literacy: Maximizing Children's Investments in School Learning." Paper presented at the *Resource Teachers: Literacy Training Programme*, July 12–13.

Comber, B., P. Cormack, and J. O'Brien. 2001. Schooling Disruptions: The Case of Critical Literacy. In *The Fate of Progressive Language Policies and Practice*, ed. C.

Dudley-Marling and C. Edelsky. Urbana, IL: National Council of Teachers of English.

Comber, B., and B. Kamler. 1997. "Critical Literacies: Politicizing the Language Classroom." *Interpretations*, 30(1): 30–53.

Comber, B., and A. Simpson, eds. 2001. *Negotiating Critical Literacies in Classrooms*. Mahwah, NJ: Lawrence Erlbaum Associates.

Comber, B., and P. Thompson. 2002. Critical Literacy, Social Action and Children's Representations of "Place." Paper presented at the *American Educational Research Association* conference. New Orleans.

Delpit, L. 1995. *Other People's Children: Cultural Conflict in the Classroom*. New York: New Press.

DeNavas-Walt, C., B. D. Proctor, and C. H. Lee. 2005. *Income, Poverty, and Health Insurance Coverage in the United States: 2004*. Washington, DC: U.S. Government Printing Office.

DeParle, J. 2004. *American Dream: Three Women, Ten Kids, and a Nation's Drive to End Welfare*. New York: Viking.

Dyson, A. H. 1993. *Social Worlds of Children Learning to Write in an Urban Primary School*. New York: Teachers College Press.

———. 2001. Relational Sense and Textual Sense in a U.S. Urban Classroom: The Contested Case of Emily, Girl Friend of a Ninja. In *Negotiating Critical Literacies in Classrooms,* ed. B. Comber and A. Simpson, 3–18. Mahwah, NJ: Lawrence Erlbaum Associates.

Edin, K., and M. Kefalas. 2005. *Promises I Can Keep: Why Poor Women Put Motherhood Before Marriage*. Los Angeles: University of California Press.

Ehrenreich, B. 2001. *Nickel and Dimed: On (Not) Getting By in America*. New York: Henry Holt and Company.

Epstein, D. 1993. *Changing Classroom Cultures: Anti-racism, Politics and Schools*. Stoke-on-Trent, United Kingdom: Trentham.

Estes, E. 1974. *The Hundred Dresses*. Orlando, FL: Harcourt Brace & Company.

Ewald, W., and A. Lightfoot. 2001. *I Wanna Take Me a Picture: Teaching Photography and Writing to Children*. Boston: Beacon Press.

Fairclough, N. 1995. *Critical Discourse Analysis: The Critical Study of Language*. New York: Longman.

Fehring, H., and P. Green, eds. 2001. *Critical Literacy: A Collection of Articles from the Australian Literacy Educators' Association*. Newark, DE: International Reading Association.

Finders, M. 1997. *Just Girls: Hidden Literacies and Life in Junior High*. New York: Teachers College Press.

Finn, P. 1999. *Literacy with an Attitude: Educating Working-class Children in Their Own Self-interest*. New York: State University of New York Press.

Foss, A. 2002. "Peeling the Onion: Teaching Critical Literacy with Students of Privilege." *Language Arts* 79(5): 393–403.

Foucault, M. 1990. *The History of Sexuality: An Introduction*. New York: New Press.

Freebody, P., and A. Luke. 1990. "Literacies Programs: Debates and Demands in Cultural Context." *Australian Journal of Language and Literacy* 5(7): 7–16.

Freire, P. 1970. *Pedagogy of the Oppressed*. New York: Continuum Publishing.

———. 1998. *Teachers as Cultural Workers: Letters to Those Who Dare Teach*. Boulder, CO: Westview Press.

Freire, P., and D. Macedo. 1987. *Literacy: Reading the Word and the World*. Westport, CT: Bergin & Garvey.

Freire, P., and I. Shor. 1987. *A Pedagogy for Liberation: Dialogues on Transforming Education*. Westport, CT: Bergin & Garvey.

Gans, H. 1995. *The War Against the Poor: The Underclass and Antipoverty Policy*. New York: Basic Books.

Gee, J. P. 1996. *Social Linguistics and Literacies: Ideology in Discourses*. Bristol, PA: The Falmer Press.

———. 1999. *An Introduction to Discourse Analysis: Theory and Method*. New York: Routledge.

———. 2001. "Critical Literacy/Socially Perceptive Literacy." In *Critical Literacy: A Collection of Articles from the Australian Literacy Educators' Association*, ed. H. Fehring and P. Green, 15–39. Newark, DE: International Reading Association.

Giroux, H. 2004. "Neoliberalism and the Demise of Democracy: Resurrecting Hope in Dark Times." In *Dissident Voice,* retrieved April 3, 2006, from www.dissidentvoice.org/Aug04/Giroux0807.htm.

Giroux, H., C. Lankshear, and P. McLaren, eds. 1996. *Counternarratives: Cultural Studies in Critical Pedagogies in Postmodern Spaces*. New York: Routledge.

Graves, D. 1994. *A Fresh Look at Writing*. Portsmouth, NH: Heinemann.

Halperin, R. 1998. *Practicing Community: Class, Culture, and Power in an Urban Neighborhood.* Austin, TX: The University of Texas Press.

Heath, S. B. 1983. *Ways with Words: Language, Life and Work in Communities and Classrooms*. New York: Cambridge University Press.

Heffernan, L. 2004. *Critical Literacy and Writer's Workshop: Bringing Purpose and Passion to Student Writing*. Newark, DE: International Reading Association.

Heffernan, L., and M. Lewison. 2003. "Social Narrative Writing: (Re)constructing Kid Culture in the Writer's Workshop." *Language Arts* 80(6): 435–44.

———. 2005. "What's Lunch Got to Do with It? Critical Literacy and the Discourse of the Lunchroom." *Language Arts* 83(2): 107–18.

Hicks, D. 2001. "Literacies and Masculinities in the Life of a Young Working-class Boy." *Language Arts* 78(3): 217–26.

———. 2001. *Reading Lives: Working-class Children and Literacy Learning*. New York: Teachers College Press.

———. 2004. "Back to Oz? Rethinking the Literary in a Critical Study of Reading." *Research in the Teaching of English* 39(1): 63–84.

hooks, b. 1994. *Teaching to Transgress: Education as the Practice of Freedom*. New York: Routledge.

———. 1996. *Bone Black: Memories of Girlhood*. New York: Henry Holt and Company.

———. 2000a. *Where We Stand: Class Matters*. New York: Routledge.

———. 2000b. *Feminist Theory: From Margin to Center*. Cambridge, MA: South End Press.

International Centre of Prison Studies. "World Prison Population List (Sixth Edition)." Retrieved May 5, 2006, from www.prisonstudies.org.

Irwin, J. 1985. *The Jail: Managing the Underclass in American Society*. Berkeley: University of California Press.

Janks, H. 2000. "Domination, Access, Diversity and Design." *Educational Review* 52(2): 175–86.

Jones, S. 2003/2004. "Writing Identities: The Identity Construction of a First Grade Girl Writer." *Ohio Journal of English Language Arts* 44(1): 24–32.

Jones, S. 2004. "Living Poverty and Literacy Learning: Sanctioning the Topics of Students' Lives." *Language Arts* 81(6): 461–69.

Joseph, L. 2002. *The Color of My Words*. New York: HarperCollins Publishers.

Kamler, B. 2001. *Relocating the Personal: A Critical Writing Pedagogy*. Albany: State University of New York Press.

Kempe, A. 1993. "No Single Meaning: Empowering Students to Construct Socially Critical Readings of Text." *Australian Journal of Language and Literacy* 16(4): 375–95.

Keyssar, A. 2005. "Reminders of Poverty, Soon Forgotten." *The Chronicle of Higher Education*, B6–B8.

Kohl, H. 1996. *Should We Burn Babar? Essays on Children's Literature and the Power of Stories*. New York: New Press.

Lankshear, C., and P. McLaren. 1993. *Critical Literacy: Politics, Praxis, and the Postmodern*. New York: SUNY.

Lareau, A. 1989, 2000. *Home Advantage: Social Class and Parental Intervention in Elementary Education*. New York: Rowman & Littlefield.

Lensmire, T. 1994. *When Children Write: Critical Re-visions of the Writing Workshop*. New York: Teachers College Press.

———. 2000. *Powerful Writing, Responsible Teaching*. New York: Teachers College Press.

Lewis, C. 2000. "Critical Issues: Limits of Identification: The Personal, Pleasurable, and Critical in Reader Response." *Journal of Literacy Research* 32(2): 253–68.

Luke, A., and P. Freebody. 1996. Critical Literacy and the Question of Normativity: An Introduction. In *Constructing Critical Literacies: Teaching and Learning Textual Practice*, ed. S. Muspratt, A. Luke, and P. Freebody, 1–13. Creskill, NJ: Hampton Press.

———. 1999. "Further Notes on the Four Resources Model." *Reading Online*, www.readingonline.org/research/lukefreebody.html.

Luttrell, W. 1997. *School-smart and Mother-wise: Working-class Women's Identity and Schooling*. New York: Routledge

———. 2003. *Pregnant Bodies, Fertile Minds: Gender, Race, and the Schooling of Pregnant Teens*. New York: Routledge.

Lyon, G. E. 1999. *Where I'm From: Where Poems Come From*. Spring, TX: Absey & Co.

Macedo, D. 1994. Preface. In *Politics of Liberation: Paths from Freire*, ed. P. McLaren and C. Lankshear, xiii–xviii. New York: Routledge.

MacLeod, J. 1995. *Ain't No Makin' It: Aspirations and Attainment in a Low-income Neighborhood*. Boulder, CO: Westview Press.

Maloney, M., and C. Auffrey. 2004. *The Social Areas of Cincinnati: An Analysis of Social*

Needs. Cincinnati, OH: School of Planning, University of Cincinnati; UC Institute for Community Partnerships.

McLaren, P. (2006). "Critical Literacy Reloaded." Keynote presentation at Threat-n-Youth Cultural Studies Conference. New York, Teachers College, Columbia University.

McLaren, P., and C. Lankshear, eds. 1994. *Politics of Liberation: Paths from Freire.* New York: Routledge.

Meyerhoff, M. 2004. "Head Lice—An Equal Opportunity Infestation?" Retrieved December 10, 2005, from www.findarticles.com/p/articles/mi_m0816/is_2_21/ai_n6191122.

Muspratt, S., A. Luke, and P. Freebody, eds. 1997. *Constructing Critical Literacies: Teaching and Learning Textual Practice.* Creskill, NJ: Hampton Press.

O'Brien, J. 2001. Children Reading Critically: A Local History. In *Negotiating Critical Literacies in Classrooms,* ed. B. Comber and A. Simpson, 37–54. Mahwah, NJ: Lawrence Erlbaum Associates.

Obermiller, P. 1996. *Down Home Down Town: Urban Appalachians Today.* Dubuque, IA: Kendall/Hunt.

———. 1999. "Paving the Way." In *Backtalk from Appalachia Confronting Stereotypes,* ed. D. B. Billings, G. Norman, and K. Ledford, 251–66. Lexington: University Press of Kentucky.

Philliber, W., and C. McCoy. 1981. *The Invisible Minority: Urban Appalachians.* Lexington: The University Press of Kentucky.

Powell, R., S. Cantrell, and S. Adams. 2001. "Saving Black Mountain: The Promise of Critical Literacy in a Multicultural Democracy." *The Reading Teacher* 54(8): 772–82.

Reay, D. 1998. *Class Work: Mothers' Involvement in Their Children's Primary Schooling.* London: UCL Press.

Rich, A. 1981. *Of Woman Born: Motherhood as Experience and Institution.* New York: Bantam Books.

Rist, R. 2000. "Student Social Class and Teacher Expectations: The Self-fulfilling Prophecy in Ghetto Education." *Harvard Educational Review* 70: 257–301.

Rogers, R. 2003. *A Critical Discourse Analysis of Family Literacy Practices: Power in and Out of Print.* Mahwah, NJ: Lawrence Erlbaum Associates.

Rose, M. 1989. *Lives on the Boundary: A Moving Account of the Struggles and Achievements of America's Educational Underclass.* New York: Penguin.

———. 2004. *The Mind at Work: Valuing the Intelligence of the American Worker.* New York: Penguin.

Rothstein, R. 2004. *Class and Schools: Using Social, Economic, and Educational Reform to Close the Black-White Achievement Gap.* New York: Economic Policy Institute.

Rylant, C. 1982. *When I Was Young in the Mountains.* New York: Dutton Juvenile.

———. 1996. *Henry and Mudge Get the Cold Shivers.* New York: Aladdin.

———. 1997. *Henry and Mudge and the Best Day of All.* New York: Aladdin.

Sahni, U. 2001. "Children Appropriating Literacy: Empowerment Pedagogy from Young Children's Perspective." In *Negotiating Critical Literacies in Classrooms,* ed. B. Comber and A. Simpson, 19–36. Mahwah, NJ: Lawrence Erlbaum Associates.

Santiago, E. 1993. *When I Was Puerto Rican*. New York: Vintage.

Schneider, J. 2001. "No Blood, Guns or Gays Allowed!: The Silencing of the Elementary Writer." *Language Arts* 78:415–25.

Schwartz, T. 2002. Write Me: A Participatory Action Research Project with Urban Appalachian Girls. Ed.D. diss., University of Cincinnati.

Scieszka, J. 1989. *The True Story of the 3 Little Pigs By A. Wolf*. New York, Penguin Group.

Scott, J., and D. Leonhardt. 2005. Shadowy Lines That Still Divide. *New York Times,* sect. 1, p. A1.

Sennett, R., and J. Cobb. 1972. *The Hidden Injuries of Class*. New York: W. W. Norton & Company.

Skinner, E. 2006. Teenage Addiction: Adolescent Girls Drawing upon Popular Culture Texts as Mentors for Writing in an After-school Writing Club. Ed.D. diss., New York: Teachers College, Columbia University.

Smith, D. 1997. *The Conceptual Practices of Power: A Feminist Sociology of Knowledge*. Toronto: University of Toronto Press.

Steedman, C. 1982. *The Tidy House: Little Girls Writing*. London: Virago Press.

Street, B. 2003. "What's 'New' in New Literacy Studies? Critical Approaches to Literacy in Theory and Practice." *Current Issues in Comparative Education* 5(2).

———. 2005. "At Last: Recent Applications of New Literacy Studies in Educational Contexts." *Research in the Teaching of English* 39(4): 417–23.

Tough, P. 2001. "The Alchemy of OxyContin." *New York Times Magazine*. Retrieved July 29, 2001, from http://query.nytimes.com/gst/fullpage.html?sec=health&res=9403E2DF113AF93AA15754C0A9679C8B63.

Vasquez, V. 2004. *Negotiating Critical Literacies with Young Children*. Mahwah, NJ: Lawrence Erlbaum Associates.

Wallowitz, L. 2004. "Reading as Resistance: Gendered Messages in Literature and Media." *English Journal* 93(3): 26–31.

Walkerdine, V. 1998. *Counting Girls Out: Girls and Mathematics*. Bristol, MA:Falmer Press.

Walkerdine, V., H. Lucey, and J. Melody. 2001. *Growing Up Girl: Psychosocial Explorations of Gender and Class*. New York: New York University Press.

Weedon, C. 1997. *Feminist Practice and Poststructuralist Theory*. Malden, MA: Blackwell.

Weiler, K. 1994. Freire and a Feminist Pedagogy of Difference. In *Politics of Liberation: Paths from Freire,* ed. P. McLaren and C. Lankshear, 12–40. New York: Routledge.

White, C. 2001. Examining Poverty and Literacy in our Schools: Janice's Story. In *Critiquing Whole Language and Classroom Inquiry,* ed. S. Boran and B. Comber, 168–98. Urbana, IL: National Council of Teachers of English.

Wilkerson, I. 2005. "Angela Whitiker's Climb." *New York Times.* Retrieved June 12, 2005, from www.nytimes.com/2005/06/12/national/class/ANGELA-FINAL.html?ei=5090&en=cd0384dc26a867d7&ex=1276228800&partner=rssuserland&emc=rss&pagewanted=print.

Williams, V. B. 2001. *Amber Was Brave, Essie Was Smart*. New York: Scholastic.

Wortham, S. 2001. "Interactionally Situated Cognition: A Classroom Example." *Cognition Science* 25:37–66.

Index

heroin, 19–20
hillbillies. *See* White Trash
hillbilly heroin, 19
home visits, 110
hooks, bell, 63–65, 66, 89, 100n, 130
Horton, Myles, 63, 66, 131
huffing, 19, 21n
Hundred Dresses, The, 12
Hurricane Katrina, 45–47

I Am From, 5–6, 8–10
ideal mother, 102–3
identities
    classism and, 1–10
    consciousness, hybrid, and, 10
    deconstruction of, 75–76, 78
    mothering, 89–98, 150
    personal history and, 2–5
    poverty and, 23
    reconstruction of, 76–78, 150, 155
    as shaped by society, xvii–xviii, 158–59
integration, forced, 63–64
invisible minority, 19

jail, 40–43
Janks, Hilary, 64
Jones, Stephanie, x–xi, 58–59, 152–55
journals, home-school weekly, 109
justice system. *See* criminal justice system

Kamler, B., 65
Kohl, Herbert, 112

Lensmire, Timothy, 133
life
    privileged, 25
    writing from, 2–10
Lightfoot, Alexandra, 130
literacy. *See* critical literacy
literature. *See also* texts
    deconstructing children's, 128–29
    multicultural, 128
Louisiana, at home in, 154–55
Lucey, H., 99, 103, 105
Luke, Allan, 113
luxuries presented as necessities, 23–24
Lyons, George Ella, 2, 6, 7

Macedo, Donaldo, 8, 24, 131
magazine, literary, 143–50
margins, lives on the, 13–14, 22–33,
        34–44, 62, 79, 81–83, 131–32,
        160–61
marijuana, 19–20
media images, 13–14, 23–24, 27–29,
        60–61, 127
meetings, community, 110
Melody, June, 99, 103, 105

memoir, 6–7
metaphor, 15, 143
migration, pattern of, 18–19
minority, invisible, 19
Miss Nelson Is Missing!, 128–29
modeled writing, 6–7
mother
    desire to, 90–98
    ideal, 102–3
mothers
    classroom conversations and daughters,
        87–100
    identities as, 89–98, 150
    literacy of daughters impacted by,
        157–59
    power of, 140–41
    teachers and working-class, 90–91,
        100–11
    teen, 93–94
    working-class and daughters, 87–88,
        93–94, 97–100, 101–3, 157–59
Multicultural Trap of critical literacy, 113,
        115, 127–29
My Brother, 143
My Friend's Window, 15
My Home, 16

narratives about marriage and children,
        96–100
natural, challenging what seems to be,
        59–61
necessities, luxuries presented by, 23–24
negotiated power, 83–85
New York Times, 45
No Child Left Behind, vii
normal, perspective of what is, 79–80
notes, positive, 110

open-door policy in classroom, 109
opportunity, windows of, 152–63
oppressors, 36
Ortner, Sherry, 45
ourselves, look into, 1–10
overcoming, conversation about, 22–23
OxyContin, 19

parent-teacher conferences, 108, 109–10
partnership between schools and families,
        107–11
pedagogy centering on student lives, 5,
        62–66, 128–29, 131–33
peer relations, impact on writing, 133
perspective
    critical literacy and, 35–36, 65, 67, 71,
        73–75, 79–80, 84, 115, 158
    in-school reform and, 160–63
    social class and, 59, 111
    in texts, 127, 129